Sid Vicious

Rock 'n' roll star

Sid Vicious

Rock 'n' roll star

Malcolm Butt

Plexus, London

This book is dedicated to my brother, Stuart, whose support, encouragement and inspiration will never be forgotten.

Published by Plexus Publishing Limited
55a Clapham Common Southside
London SW4 9BX
Tel: 020 7622 2440
Fax: 020 7622 2441
www.plexusbooks.com

British Library Cataloguing in Publication Data

Butt, Malcolm
    Sid Vicious : rock 'n' roll star
    1. Vicious, Sid, 2. Rock musicians – Great
    Britain – Biography
    I. Title
    782 . 4'2166'092

    ISBN 0 85965 340 4

Printed by Bell & Bain Ltd, Glasgow
Designed by The Design Revolution, Brighton

ACKNOWLEDGEMENTS

We would like to thank the following for help in
research, assembling visual material and supplying pho-
tographs: British Film Institute; CarolineCoon/Camera
Press; Camera Press; Jean Constant Gindreau; the *Daily
Mirror*; Walt Davidson; photographs from *The Sid Vicious
Family Album* courtesy Anne Beverley; Glitterbest; Bob
Gruen/Starfile; The Hulton Getty Picture Collection Ltd;
John Ingham; Bob Leafe/Topix Inc; Mirror Syndication
International; Dennis Morris for the cover photograph,
and photographs on pages 42, 52, 61, 71, 74/75, 76,
77, 78/79, 80, 82, 83, 123 (copyright © 1997 by Dennis
Morris); Denis O'Regan; Barry Plummer; Popperfoto;
Mercury Records; Erica Echenberg/Redferns; John
Tiberi/Redferns; Richie Aaron/Redferns; Jamie Reid; Mick
Rock; Sire Records; Ray Stevenson; Fred and Judy
Vermorel's book, *Sex Pistols: the Inside Story*; Gavin
Walsh's collection; Annette Weatherman; EMI Records;
Warner Bros Records; Virgin Records; Palace Pictures
and Zenith Films.
    We also wish to acknowledge the following books:
Sid's Way by Keith Bateson and Alan Parker; *The Wicked
Ways of Malcolm McLaren* by Craig Bromberg; *The Boy
Looked at Johnny* by Julie Burchill and Tony Parsons;
1988: the New Wave Punk Rock Explosion by Caroline
Coon; *DOA: the Official Film Book*; *In the Gutter* by Val
Hennessy; *I Was a Teenage Sex Pistol* by Glen Matlock;
12 Days on the Road: the Sex Pistols and America by
Noel E. Monk and Jimmy Guterman; *New Wave
Explosion* by Myles Palmer; *England's Dreaming* by Jon
Savage; *Sex Pistols: Agents of Anarchy* by Tony Scrivener;
Impresario: Malcolm McLaren and the British New Wave
by Paul Taylor; *Shockwave* by Virginia Boston; *Sex Pistols:
the Inside Story* by Fred and Judy Vermorel; *The Sex
Pistols Diary: Sex Pistols Day by Day* by Lee Wood; *The
Sid Vicious Family Album* by Ann Beverley.
    Special thanks to the following people and publica-
tions: Jamie Reid for his Sex Pistols designs; Malcolm
McLaren and Virgin Records; *Creem*; the *Daily Mail*; the
Daily Mirror; the *Evening Standard*; the *Face*; *High Times*;
the *Los Angeles Times*; *Melody Maker*; the *New Musical
Express*; the *New York Times*; *Record Mirror*; *Rolling Stone*;
Slash; *Sounds*; the *Sun*; the *Times*; *Trouser Press*; *Twisted*;
ZigZag.
    It has not been possible in all cases to trace the
copyright sources, and the publishers would be glad to
hear from any such unacknowledged copyright holders.

contents

chapter 1

"Sid actually did nothing. Sid was a coathanger."

John Lydon, 1996

When the Sex Pistols finally reformed in 1996, it was inevitable that Sid Vicious would be mentioned. Since his death some 18 years previously, Sid had increasingly come to be seen as the visual embodiment of punk rock; the ultimate Sex Pistol and a modern-day cult hero. At the packed press conference at Oxford Street's 100 Club, John Lydon (formerly Johnny Rotten), was in characteristically uncharitable mood when it was suggested that the Sex Pistols were incomplete without Sid. As he rightly pointed out, in the intervening years, speculation, exaggeration, misinformation and sheer mythologising have elevated Sid Vicious to the status of a rock icon. The actual events frequently suggest a very different reality.

By the age of five, Sid, aka Simon John Ritchie, had already experienced more upheaval and travel than some people do in a lifetime. His first major excursion, with his doting mother Anne, was to Ibiza, the southernmost of the three main Balearic islands off the east coast of Spain, which also include Menorca and Majorca. Having joined the Royal Air Force at 18, Anne Randall had met John Ritchie and set up home together in Lee Green, south-east London, although they never got married. At first, everything went well, but with the birth of a son, christened John Simon Ritchie, in May 1957, John Ritchie displayed little willingness to assume the parental responsibility that this addition to the family brought. Shortly afterwards, Ritchie abdicated from his role altogether by leaving Anne, who was left to fend for the new-born alone, with occasional help from Ritchie's parents in Dagenham.

Sid, punk icon and ultimate Sex Pistol, at the peak of the Pistols' fame.

The young Simon was the image of his absent father, but tended towards his mother in character, picking up her love for music in a house full of the sounds of jazz, in particular Ella Fitzgerald. As a toddler, Simon would clatter his mother's spoons on battered saucepans in a comical attempt at drumming. By the time Simon was three, Anne had her trip to Ibiza planned as a break from the gruelling single-parent life she was struggling with at home. Initially the sun-baked sojourn provided an idyllic holiday, spent cycling round the picturesque island, but when the promised maintenance payments from Simon's father failed to materialise from England, the Balearic experience soon became a nightmare of bad debt and unpaid rent. With the help of some charitable American ex-pats living on the island and a local community enamoured of the quirky English woman and her energetic son, Anne managed to cope for two years before eventually being forced to accept defeat and return to London. Once back in the capital, she was free of the bad debts and angry landlords, but the difficulties abroad had exposed the weaknesses in her relationship with Simon's father. Not only had he not sent any money, but his promised visit to Ibiza had

At the age of three, with mother Anne Beverley, in sunny Ibiza, 1960. The idyllic holiday was, sadly, not to last.

never materialised either. With that affair in tatters, Anne found herself as a single mother with a young child, who already knew how to swear loudly in Spanish.

After the Ibiza trip had turned sour, Anne returned to London, living first with her mother for a while before packing her bags again to lodge in an old house in Balham. Her very elderly land-lady led a reclusive and house-bound lifestyle, which provided Anne with the lux-ury of a residential baby-sitter, allowing her to venture out and earn a living. Anne got a job at Ronnie Scott's jazz club in Soho and worked long night hours before returning home to spend the waking day with Simon, who shared his time between the maternal landlady, his mum and brief visits to the Rudolph Stein Nursery. This arrangement worked well, but Anne soon tired of all the travelling from south London, and so with some financial help from her

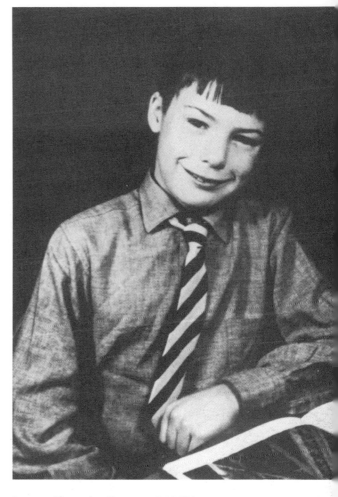

As a smiling schoolboy, aged 11. Taken at Sandrock Road Secondary Modern School in Tunbridge Wells, 1968.

mother and sister, she moved once more, this time into a flat in Covent Garden's Drury Lane. In exchange for the commuting convenience, she had to put up with gas lighting, a corridor open to the elements, an outside toi-let and no running hot water. While they lived here Simon attended the Soho primary school.

This was to be the first of many schools that Simon attended, as his child-hood became a blur of changed lodgings, new schoolmates and strange sur-roundings. His time at this first school in cosmopolitan Soho was brief and troubled. At home he found solace in his Action men figures. He was naturally something of a loner – his reticence to join in was hardened by the bullying he experienced when he went through a nervous twitching phase, and his mother's disgust at the school's reluctance to act meant his days at this school were numbered.

Next they moved near to the American Embassy in Grosvenor Square, where Simon wore his first formal uniform, complete with blazer, shorts and school tie. Then it was up-sticks to Oxford, a move further afield that brought unexpected romance into Anne's life. She met a charming man, Chris Beverley, in the city of spires, and after a whirlwind courtship, they were married. Their relationship was bonded by the fact that Chris loved Simon and Anne was delighted when her new husband made a formal request to legally adopt his stepson. Unfortunately, tragedy struck months later when Chris died of ill health before the adoption went through. Anne and Simon were alone once again.

Anne next moved to Tunbridge Wells in an attempt to make a clean break from the tragedy behind them in Oxford, and for the next six years she and Simon enjoyed relative stability. Chris Beverley came from a stable, well-off family and his grieving parents paid for Simon to attend a private school, where he would board during the week, and then looked after him at weekends at the family home in Wadhurst, while Anne lived and worked in Tunbridge Wells. By now, however, Simon was developing something of an individual character. He owned a television but made it known he thought it was a waste of time. He enjoyed some of his educational life, but struggled to endure the discipline demanded by so many private schools, and did not appear to be overly academic. He really made his mark when he told the horrified school elders that he no longer believed in God. At this stage, he was also starting to experiment with his sexuality: "I had a phase of dressing up in women's clothes when I was about 14 or 15. I only did it for a couple of months though. I'm not very interested in straight sex, I like perversions."

Simon attended educational establishments of various kinds in Tunbridge Wells, Sandown, Bristol, Stamford Hill and finally Stoke Newington. It was to Stamford Hill that Anne took him after yet more money troubles had ended the stable life enjoyed in Tunbridge Wells.

Simon left school with two O levels in English Literature and English Language and absolutely no ambition to pursue his academic studies. His first paid job was as a dogsbody and trainee cutter at the Simpson's factory in Kingsland Road, east London, making the pockets for Daks slacks, but this lasted only a matter of weeks as he was sacked for consistently shoddy work. After several aborted odd jobs, Simon decided to go back into education, albeit on a vocational photography course at Hackney College of Further Education.

Despite being largely non-academic, Simon loved the art and history classes, and examples of his work were accomplished and promising. As with the private school in Tunbridge Wells, however, he had great difficulty being told what to do and as a result lasted only two terms at Hackney. Even so, it had been worth it – while he was there, his life had changed in many ways. He had come out of his shell somewhat, he had developed a passion for David Bowie and he had discovered the joys of clothing and fashion. He had also made some new friends, not least a long-haired, young, skinny Irish boy called John Joseph Lydon.

Anne Beverley remembers John Lydon when he first came round the house to visit her son, as she told Jon Savage in *England's Dreaming*: "He had hair down to here, a beautiful head. He was shy. If I just looked at him he went beetroot red. Couldn't say a word. I'd never met someone that shy before." His shyness and long hair soon vanished as his college career began – within months he had hacked off his locks at home and, in an ill-fated attempt to dye it yellow, Lydon had turned his barnet a dirty green. At college he adopted a disaffected demeanour and sharpened his already rampant cynicism by revelling in everything his background opposed. His behaviour appalled his orthodox Catholic family – when he was bought a nice suit in a bid to tidy him up, he immediately vanished upstairs and

The curly-permed 18-year-old art student and Bolan fan: at Hackney College, 1975.

Still in glam-rock mode: at Hackney College, 1975.

returned some time later with the suit cut to ribbons and re-tailored with a motley collection of safety pins. Lydon was thrown out of the house.

Simon Beverley (he had taken to using his more loving stepfather's surname) was a year younger than Lydon and found himself instantly drawn to this skinny, fiercely independent rogue. Simon had himself begun dyeing his hair in imitation of his hero David Bowie. It was now late 1972 and over the next two years glam rock became the chosen music of thousands of youngsters. Simon was amongst those who rejected the overblown but prevalent prog-rock scene (epitomised by such bands as Emerson, Lake and Palmer and Yes, both revered by contemporary critics) for this less studied form. With David Bowie and Marc Bolan as the key proponents, glam rock soon entered the charts, with hits by bands such as the Sweet, Mud and the all-conquering Slade. These were all acts who exaggerated the sartorial over-emphasis of psychedelia and played down the sometimes overly intellectual side of rock. It was loud, it was fun and it was immensely popular.

Sid was particularly fascinated with Ziggy Stardust, the David Bowie pseudo-alien creation who had swept up the UK in a fever of face paint and futuristic clothing. After struggling for some years, Bowie's alter ego finally brought fame with the enormous impact of *The Rise and Fall of Ziggy Stardust and the Spiders from Mars* concept album. Even when Bowie officially and publicly retired Ziggy in 1974, the highly individual look remained popular for some time, and Simon Beverley loved it. He dyed his hair red and, in a desperate attempt to get his hair to stick up like Ziggy's, would hold his head upside down in the oven, while a laughing John Lydon timed him for exactly twenty minutes.

Simon's bedroom walls were plastered with posters of Bowie, he bought the records religiously and attended as many concerts as he could afford. The effeminate look was vital to this obsession and Simon adopted the camp style completely – he wore bright varnish on his toe-nails and wandered around the snow covered streets of east London in sandals to show off his stylish feet. He regularly bought music and fashion magazines by the dozen and poorly attempted to recreate what he saw within those pages. After Bowie came Bolan, and with Simon now a fully fledged fashion victim, a large curly perm soon adorned his head.

When Lydon was thrown out of the family home, Simon was also asked to do the same. His mum had acquired an eleventh floor council flat which she really loved, and since Sid's increasingly brash character was beginning to prove difficult to cope with, the two mutually agreed to live apart for a while. Simon joined Lydon in a squat in Hampstead behind the station, and as one of the first independent moves in his life, he changed his name to Sid Vicious, albeit prompted by Lydon.

The origins of what has become a legendary rock moniker seem clouded in the same sort of mythology that has come to complicate every aspect of Sid's life. Some say he was named after Lydon's pet rat. Others say that one day they thought of the worst names possible; Simon hated Sid the most and hence became the very same. The Vicious surname could have been from the same pet rat who had once bitten Lydon's father, or maybe it was exactly the opposite – as Lydon later told Alan Parker in his book *Sid's Way*: "Sid was the least vicious and least screwed-up person that I'd ever met then or have since, hence Vicious." For Simon, the name change was no problem – he had already become used to being called whatever his mum had a whim for, be it Simon Beverley, Simon Ritchie or just Simes. Sid was just another alternative and from this point on, that was his chosen tag.

The brotherly misfits Lydon and Vicious complemented each other perfectly. Sid was a loner when he came to the college but Lydon brought out the humour in him, a biting wit that many people still remember Sid for. Similarly, this humour served to lighten Lydon in his darker, more sombre moments. Neither was seriously into drinking but Sid developed an early fixation for speed, which later became the chosen drug of the punk rock movement, and soon progressed to injecting it. The first time he took drugs intravenously, he even used an old metal syringe given to him by his mother, herself an addict.

Up to this age, Sid's introverted nature and inherent anti-authority tendencies as a child suggested to some degree his later character, but there was very little to indicate he would go on to become infamous for his massive drug use and violent behaviour. The lack of a father figure certainly disrupted Sid's childhood, and when he did find one, Chris Beverley, this was taken away from him almost immediately. Sid's mother adored him and made up for his broken family background by spoiling her young son indulgently. Their transient lifestyle also encouraged Sid's waywardness, in that it prevented him from establishing any lasting friendships and relationships during his formative years. By his teens, Sid was used to looking after himself, and doing as he pleased. When drugs were added to that cocktail, the consequences were more often than not disastrous.

Even back then, the drugs brought out a much less pleasant side to Sid's otherwise amiable character. At one party in Hackney he had evidently taken too much speed and went berserk, attacking a policeman and knocking his front tooth out in the process. However, later talk of his wild womanising during this period is questionable – Lydon always believed that Nancy Spungen was Sid's first sexual encounter.

The two worked their way through various tedious day jobs and accompanying seedy squats. Neither could muster enough enthusiasm nor be tolerated by their employers to last long at each new occupation – most comical of all was a green-haired John Lydon taking a post at a children's play centre, only to be sacked after a flood of complaints from worried parents. They both worked at Cranks' health food restaurant in Tottenham Court Road for a while and Lydon also enjoyed spells at a sewage farm and a shoe shop. Another feeble source of income was from busking in underground stations – since Sid couldn't play the acoustic guitar he owned, nor Lydon the violin under his neck, the screeching racket they produced was never very profitable, made worse by the fact they only played one Alice Cooper song over and over again.

When they were out of work and short of money, Sid often paid their way by selling small amounts of speed. After a while he also started to drink heavily. Inevitably, they got into scrapes, and started frequenting gay discos where they claimed they received less grief from the more liberal-minded clientele. Sid would be game for anything when he was drunk or on speed – one time he found out where Bryan Ferry lived and had to be persuaded by Lydon from going round with a bottle of Martini and demanding to be let in. Jon Savage in *England's Dreaming* suggests that Sid even flirted with prostitution as a means of making money during this period.

One of the places they used during this period was a flashy St. James' brothel owned by Linda Ashby, a lesbian prostitute who earned a sizeable living thrashing various high society types and politicians. It was this sleazy base that became the meeting point for the inner circle of the later Sex Pistols. Part of this inner circle was a group of lads known as the Four Johns. This consisted of Sid and John Lydon, along with John Wardle, latterly known as Jah Wobble or Wobble the Thug, and John Gray. Throughout 1974–5, they would venture down to Chelsea to drunkenly terrorise the jet set and frequent the handful of cutting-edge boutiques that were cropping up in the King's Road. With their technicolor hair (John Gray's was lilac, Lydon's was green and Sid's was plastered with vaseline and talcum powder) their jumble sale clothes and their increasingly obnoxious attitude, the gang hated everything that the wealth and finery of Chelsea's jet set represented. The long hair and flares that were in vogue were loathed and frequently spat at during their chaotic walks along the road. Sometimes their contempt spilled over in to boredom and turned in on themselves, with Lydon and Sid regularly burning their arms with cigarettes.

Sex: the shop at 430 King's Road, where it all began. Jordan (left) and friend.

At the bottom of the King's Road where it turned into the less trendy quarter of World's End, the Four Johns found a shop that absolutely fascinated them. At this time it went by the name of Too Fast To Live, Too Young To Die, but shortly after, its owners Malcolm McLaren and Vivienne Westwood changed the entire decor of the shop and its stock, and simplified the name to just Sex, and in so doing created the crucible for the most inflammatory band of the decade, perhaps ever.

chapter

"They are Dickensian-like
urchins   who
    with ragged clothes
    and pock
    marked
    faces roam the
        streets of foggy gas-lit
                London pillaging.

    Some of these
    ragamuffin gangs

    jump on tables amidst the

    charred debris and with burning debris
        play rock'n'roll to the
        screaming delight
            of the frenzied,
                    pissing
                    pogoing mob...

    one of these gangs call themselves the
SEX PISTOLS"

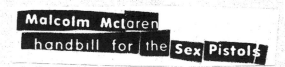

Malcolm McLaren
handbill for the Sex Pistols

Sid, still honing his punk look, at an early Clash gig.

Sid Vicious

When Wally Nightingale formed a band in 1973 he could never have imagined the impact that group would have just two full years later, nor, no doubt, would he have been pleased to know that by then he would have been sacked. Nightingale recruited school friends Paul Cook and ex-skinhead Steve Jones to help him play the Who, Small Faces, Kinks and Stooges covers that were to comprise the majority of their repertoire. Cook got hold of a second-hand Olympic drum kit with some meagre savings, while self-styled front man Jones chose alternative methods of equipping the band. Jones was an established, barely literate, self-confessed kleptomaniac, and he used his skills to furnish the band with gear. His most brash haul was a massive stash of top line gear stolen in the middle of the night from the Hammersmith Odeon stage, where none other than David Bowie had been playing a series of shows. Over the next year the band started rehearsing, with an ever changing line-up of multi-instrumentalists that fluctuated around the original founding threesome. Dressed in Hush Puppies and sounding like the Small Faces, the band practised at 533 King's Road, near Meravian corner.

At the same time they became involved with Too Fast To Live, Too Young To Die, 430 King's Road. Co-owner, Malcolm McLaren, was in his midtwenties and had grown up in the fashion business thanks to his Jewish father, who had owned a clothing factory in London. Despite being badly behaved at school, McLaren took to college life, and with the help of hand-

Vivienne Westwood and Malcolm McLaren: proprietors of Sex, and movers and shakers of punk rock.

outs from both the council and his grandmother, he spent six years doing various courses at London's art schools, starting at the famous St Martins. He loved the melting pot of ideas he found in this liberal environment, and went on to christen art schools as "islands of the dispossessed".

McLaren thrived in the libertarian atmosphere of the students' sixties and it was through this experimentation that he met Vivienne Westwood, five years his senior and running away from a failed marriage. She was a teacher and soon moved in with him, giving birth to a son in 1967. Four years later they opened their first memorabilia shop at 430 King's Road, called Let It Rock, featuring all McLaren's favourites from the fifties, such as Eddie Cochran, Billy Fury and Gene Vincent.

Let It Rock had been a haven for teddy boys with their drape jackets, brothel creeper shoes, skinny ties and drainpipe trousers; now McLaren's Too Fast To Live... ethic began attracting teenagers, amongst them the half-formed band of Cook, Jones and Nightingale. McLaren took to these three regulars, and after Jones had plagued him to help their band, he arranged a rehearsal spot for them in Covent Garden. They didn't like the new room, but it showed McLaren's penchant for managerial style. By now McLaren was hooked, and furthered his involvement by recruiting budding art school student and bassist from the suburbs Glen Matlock, his shop's Saturday boy. Matlock had impressed in the audition with a solid rendition of the Faces 'Three Button Hand-Me-Down' in Wally's bedroom.

After honing their rough sound at some BBC studios that Wally's father was re-wiring, the band christened themselves the Swankers and arranged their first gig at a flat above Tom Salter's café at 205 King's Road. The facts are unclear, but for some reason they were probably named the Strand for this show, and performed only three songs – Junior Walker and the All Stars sixties classic 'I'm A Road Runner', then the Small Faces 'Watcha Gonna Do About It?' before an original song called 'Scarface'. It was early 1975.

McLaren's priority was always the development of his shop, and on one occasion in 1973 he set off for New York where he had been invited to take part in a clothes convention. While he was there he came across the New York Dolls, who at the time were the toast of the New York scene with their camp glam punk outfits and furious style. By 1975, however, various members were struggling against drug and alcohol addiction and the band as a whole was suffering from a growing disinterest from the public. McLaren had originally been very impressed and shocked by these cross-dressing, high energy, Warhol-influenced rockers, and now in their moment of need he agreed to manage them.

He stayed in New York for six months, during which time he tried to re-launch the band as communist agitators, complete with hammer and sickle, red costumes and the slogan "What are the politics of boredom?" Unfortunately, he was trying to revive a dying corpse of a band and his efforts were doomed to fail. Their time was up and they had already been superseded by more cerebral-type musicians such as Patti Smith and Television. The band split and McLaren returned to London, undeterred by his experience and determined to put into practice the myriad of ideas he now had, using the Swankers as his guinea pig. This could be an ideal vehicle to promote his shop as well as a chance to test out the ideas he had struggled with so valiantly with the Dolls. On his return his new focus was evident, as this comment about the first New York Dolls song he heard reveals: "I thought it was the worst record I'd ever heard, [but] it didn't matter that the music was so bad. What mattered was that they were so good at being bad."

The flamboyantly-attired New York Dolls, whom Malcolm McLaren managed, briefly, prior to the Sex Pistols.

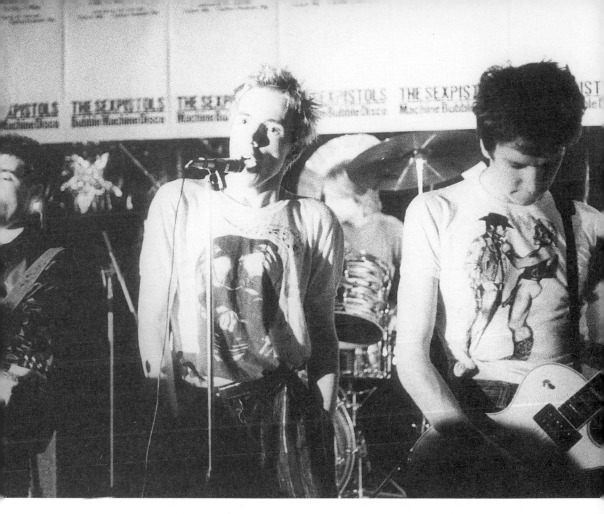

An early performance by the Sex Pistols. The pre-Sid line-up was (left to right) Glen Matlock (bass); Johnny Rotten (vocals); Paul Cook (drums); Steve Jones (guitar).

The first thing he changed back in Britain was the name the Swankers. The band had liked Kid Gladlove or the Strand, but McLaren preferred Kutie Jones and His Sex Pistols (he even printed T-shirts with this on), which was soon truncated to just the Sex Pistols. He claimed he stole this name from an infamous New York street gang.

The next change was to sack Wally Nightingale, who had formed the band in the first place. His face just did not fit for McLaren, so Jones informed him he was out at the next rehearsal, and subsequently Jones assumed the role of lead guitar. There was one more major change – Too Fast To Live... was dramatically refurbished, the old teddy boy stock shoved in a corner and the new rubber, leather and fetish gear shop adorned with a new title – Sex. It was to be McLaren's command central. All they needed now was a new front man.

Richard Hell of Television, Midge Ure (later of Slik and Ultravox), Chrissie Hynde of the Pretenders, and even McLaren himself, were supposed, possible contenders for the role. That was until John Lydon, complete with a "I Hate Pink Floyd" T-shirt and rancid green hair, walked into Sex one Saturday afternoon in August 1975. His aura of total boredom and apparent contempt for everything, combined with his peculiar looks and aggressive manner, made him a striking customer. Even amongst the various rubber and leather fetish gear that Sex had now taken to selling, Lydon seemed incapable of enthusiasm. Over the next few weeks, Lydon chatted to Cook, Jones and Matlock who were all doing part-time work at the shop, and after a while he was asked by McLaren if he wanted to sing for the band.

An audition was set up – either at Sex or at the Roebuck pub in King's Road – and an Alice Cooper song was duly murdered by Lydon's screaming, out-of- tune voice. He was immediately accepted as perfect for the Sex Pistols. Just as Simon Beverley was christened Sid Vicious by Lydon, it was now McLaren's turn to bestow his new singer with a name – Johnny Rotten. As with Sid, the origins are unclear, maybe after his constant use of that very word, maybe after his fetid and unclean teeth, maybe even after his unkempt and frankly putrid personal hygiene. This fake name trend was hijacked by punks from Andy Warhol's preference for inventing names, an idea which itself had been taken from the Hollywood film studios some decades before.

McLaren still felt the band was not complete, and so he placed an advert in the *Melody Maker* asking for a "whizz kid guitarist, not older than 20, not worse looking than Johnny Thunders, auditioning Tin Pan Alley". Steve New duly joined on guitar, as McLaren did not feel Jones was good enough on his own, but this arrangement soon fell by the wayside and the Pistols were reduced to a foursome once more – Rotten, Jones, Matlock and Cook.

Rotten's influence on the band was immediate – he took over lyric writing duties and ruffled his new colleagues' feathers with his brutally aggressive manner. However, despite their initial dislike for the newcomer, the band rehearsed well and by the winter were ready to start playing live. Their first gig with this firm line-up came at St Martin's School of Art in the West End on 6 November 1975. In a tiny upstairs room a few casual observers were witness to a debut set by a band that within eight months would have set the music world alight. On this occasion, however, an irate Social Secretary was not amused by the raucous noise and cut the power after only five songs. It was a muted start, but one that was to be indicative of the furore that the Sex Pistols were to create in the ensuing two years. The singer of the headline band Bazooka Joe, one Stuart Goddard (later Adam Ant) was so impressed by the Sex Pistols that he left his own band the very next day, claiming the Pistols' sheer brilliance had made his band seem utterly redundant. Despite this stuttering start, the Sex Pistols, it seemed, clearly had something to offer.

The musical environment into which this incendiary young band gatecrashed was a tepid and bloated world of distant superstars, over-priced stadium gigs and mammoth world tours. Led Zeppelin, David Bowie, Yes and Pink Floyd had all taken pop stars' status on to a level far removed from their fans, playing with calculated musical virtuosity in luxurious 64-track studios, and composing protracted masterpieces played on instruments that cost small fortunes. Despite this, the cocaine-riddled AOR that dominated America was still favoured by most of the British population. The charts were filled with the banality of bands like the Bay City Rollers, Paper Lace and the New Seekers. To observers stirred by the stories of the sixties pop revolution, there was nothing to suggest that this period of exciting progress hadn't come to a close. Those looking elsewhere were the young, unemployed and disaffected, unable to relate to the limousines and luxury lifestyle of the people they were supposed to aspire to. Life amongst council estates

Sid, still merely a fan and not yet a Sex Pistol, July 1976. On the right: Viv Albertine.

Not yet the centre of attention and merely in the background; Sid at an early punk gig, standing behind two punkettes.

and the Job Centres was a million miles from the powder-snorting extravagance of so many of the world's top stars. The alternatives were limited. America offered Iggy Pop, Patti Smith, Television, Talking Heads, even the fading glam of the New York Dolls. The pub rock scene was popular for its grass roots appeal, with Dr Feelgood, Graham Parker, Brinsley Schwarz and Eddie and the Hot Rods leading the scene, while reggae was also enjoying something of a peak. Otherwise there was no real outlet for the frustration that was growing with the increasingly long queues of jobless and the ever-rising inflation. McLaren seemed to sense this unrest, and spoke in prophetic terms to the *Evening Standard* when interviewed about his shop back in 1974: "I've always been involved in cults – the subterranean influence on people... I think kids have a hankering to be part of a movement. They want to be the same, to associate with a movement that's hard and tough and in the open." Even McLaren couldn't have been aware of just how rich this seam of discontent was to prove.

Add to this the cultural melting pot of Britain's art schools, vast amounts of speed and a generation of boredom and the tinder box waiting for punk was ready. The Sex Pistols appeared out of nowhere and lit the fuse. They were all under 21, Rotten carried a universal contempt, Jones was a thief with the literacy of an eight-year-old and Cook was a hard-drinking malcontent. Only Matlock had any real musical ability, but would have hardly passed an audition for one of the almighty prog rockers.

The entrance to the infamous Roxy Club, where many punk bands played, in Neal Street, Covent Garden.

After the band made steady underground progress through the end of 1975 and into 1976, the more perceptive sections of the media began to take some notice. At first there was general disinterest – after all, it could be argued the Sex Pistols were offering nothing drastically new with their music. They joined various elements from the sixties and seventies such as the Who, the Small Faces, and they stole riffs from Hawkwind, even from Mud, amid a whole amalgam of other stuff. Even the term 'punk' was stolen from aspects of American culture. The mid-sixties garage bands who tried to outdo their UK counterparts like Yes and the Yardbirds initially used the term for music, which since the 1950s had been primarily used for describing minor hoodlums as well. So, in many ways, punk was a very second-hand phenomenon. What was brand new was the focus on the attitude rather than the music, the amoral authority above musical ability which they portrayed, a slant which was to prove highly inflammable. This was summed up in Steve Jones' now famous one-liner after a riotous 1976 gig at the Marquee – "We're not into music, we're into chaos."

Over the course of 1976, the Sex Pistols gathered a fanatical, loyal, concentrated and at times highly violent following. Always at the helm of this crew was Sid Vicious, who quickly became known as their No. 1 fan, and he frequently featured in their *Anarchy in the UK* fanzine, which documented the growing scene around the band. Even before the Sex Pistols began their musical conquest, Sid was a well-known face in the King's Road. He worked at Acme Attractions,a rival store to Sex just down the road, managed by the Rastafarian DJ Don Letts who went on to mastermind the Roxy's music policy and then joined Mick Jones in Big Audio Dynamite. One Saturday morning, Bernie Rhodes, the future manager of the Clash, came into Sex chuckling about Sid Vicious. He said Sid's current girlfriend's mother had gone to the shop to complain about him and request that Sid stop seeing her daughter. In response, Sid unzipped his trousers, pulled out his dick and shouted "Get some of this" at her. Sid also spent a brief period as an assistant in Sex, but soon lost his job when he was discovered slipping a rubber T-shirt under the till to a friend.

As 1976 progressed and the Sex Pistols' notoriety grew, so did Sid's. Although he was intensely jealous of his best friend, both he and Rotten remained in close contact. On 12 December 1975, Sid went to see the Sex Pistols play at Ravensbourne College of Art in Chislehurst and from then on he was hooked. So anxious was he to see the band that he took to jumping up and down on the spot in a speed-fuelled frenzy, thus inadvertently giving birth to punk rock's very own dance, the pogo.

As more people got involved in punk and its look, Sid and Rotten became especially contemptuous of what they called "weekenders", people who dressed "normally" during the week only to adorn themselves with the latest punk fashions for the weekend festivities. Sid and Rotten hated this and ridiculed "weekenders" whenever they saw them – for these two, punk wasn't a fashion accessory, it was a way of life, an ethos which they lived every second of every day.

From the very start, the Sex Pistols refused to play the pub circuit or follow the traditional path of up-and-coming bands – they promoted themselves, played unusual venues and often didn't even book – they would simply turn up and claim they had a booking, and threaten or carry out extreme violence if the venue owner did not concede. When they needed that violent edge, Sid was always on hand. Indeed, the band and especially McLaren, encouraged this, seeing it as a sizeable asset to the Pistols' intimidating aura.

The Ramones. Sid was a big fan and adopted their trademark look of sunglasses, black leather jacket and tight ripped jeans.

At first both Rotten and Sid carried on with various day jobs – Chrissie Hynde got them some cleaning work and even earned Sid some modelling work at St Martin's. Rotten eventually gave this all up as his commitments to the Sex Pistols multiplied, and Sid's fascination with punk rock similarly grew. In the next twelve months, the Sex Pistols gigged up and down the UK, being banned from nearly every venue they played because of the damage they would cause or the violence that erupted, and in the process inspiring a whole generation of punk legends to take the call to arms, amongst them the Damned, Buzzcocks, the Clash, Penetration and Siouxsie and the Banshees. Sid was with them every step of the way.

Sid was now taking vast amounts of speed, which was often injected. He was also drinking very heavily and on his nights out at punk gigs would

Paul Cook, Steve Jones and Johnny Rotten in their loft above the rehearsal space in Denmark Street ('Tin Pan Alley'), 1976.

regularly end up in violent confrontations of one kind or another. At the Roxy, for example, a former gay club in Covent Garden's Neal Street, a speeding Sid Vicious was regularly found beating quite often innocent bystanders in the unisex toilets. After several such violent attacks, people realised he didn't take kindly to anyone who suggested that maybe he was taking too much speed. If there was no one to fight with, he would often just butt his head against the wall.

Ron Watts, who ran the 100 Club in London's Oxford Street, saw the Sex Pistols at Bucks College in High Wycombe and immediately booked them to play his venue, supporting Plummet Airlines, on 30 March 1976. Only about 50 people turned up and Rotten openly taunted Matlock on stage during a mediocre set, but Watts was so impressed that he decided to keep a close eye on the band. Sid meanwhile had just bought the Ramones' eponymous first album and like many of his contemporaries he was amazed. The Ramones had formed in March 1974, and soon secured a residency at the renowned CBGB's club in New York, where they became foremost proponents of a thriving underground scene. They dressed in black leather jackets and ripped jeans and all bore the same surname, taken from the band's name. This cartoon edge was complemented by an affected dumbness that belied the intelligence behind the façade. The highly influential *Ramones* debut long player was a high velocity mix of sixties garage-band music and straight rock'n'roll, and the whole package was highly refreshing. When that album hit the shelves in the spring of 1976, and was then followed by a UK tour in July, the Ramones influenced an entire generation of punk musicians. Sid swallowed the routine whole and took Dee Dee Ramone, their bassist, as his new hero.

Along with his love for the Ramones, Sid also nurtured a passion for any punk band. He went to every punk gig he heard about, and followed the Sex Pistols religiously. At the second of three April shows at the Nashville Club by his friend's band, Sid was accompanied by Vivienne Westwood. When she went to the toilet, a man took her seat without asking, so Sid promptly pulled a rusty bike chain out of his battered leather jacket and beat the man savagely. The fight spilled over on to the stage where the Pistols were performing, as did considerable amounts of blood, causing the band to take the rap for the fracas. This incident earned them a ban from the Nashville but also won them their first full feature in an otherwise unimpressed press, a piece in *Sounds*. Hereafter, the Sex Pistols' reputation for violence went before them and Sid was often the key to that. The band's press release had said "We hate everything" and now people were beginning to believe it.

Poised for action: Johnny Rotten on stage at the Notre Dame Hall, Soho, 1976.

By May, Ron Watts was sufficiently convinced by the Sex Pistols to offer them a residency at his 100 Club, the opening night of which came on the 11th of that month. Sid was there for every night. On tour in their battered Transit van the band demanded cash so they could afford to drive to their next gig – if a cheque was presented, trouble followed – Sid was there. If headline bands didn't allow them to borrow their gear, the band (and Sid) would rifle through their belongings while they were onstage. Sid's behaviour was like this at any punk gig. At one early Clash gig, a group of ten large, beer-swilling heavy metal fans were baiting the band and heckling them incessantly. As this continued ceaselessly, suddenly Sid ran across from the back of the stage, past the group and launched himself into the air and out on to the heads of these metal fans. After the initial advantage of surprise had worn off, Sid was beaten ferociously. For Sid, however, this did not matter – he had stood up to them and that was what counted – the inevitability of the thrashing only added to the kudos.

Sid was still great mates with Johnny Rotten. The latter had taken to wearing various articles of Westwood-designed clothing straight out of the Sex shop. On one occasion, he wore a thick rubber T-shirt to a gig supporting Kilburn and the High Roads in Walthamstow, east London, but had to take it off after the sweltering heat inside the venue made the heavy rubber a torturous garment. Sid greedily

The Sex Pistols (still with Glen Matlock in the line-up) at the Notre Dame Hall.

grabbed Rotten's cast-off and decided to wear it the next day, despite the thermometer showing 85 degrees of summer heat. Sid lasted less than an hour before he collapsed from heat exhaustion.

Back with the Sex Pistols in June, Sid was now a famous face on the scene. The band were indeed a striking visual feast, especially Rotten, whose sneering presence was all the more unnerving for the stoop he still carried from a childhood bout of spinal meningitis. Each gig would see him wear different oddities from Sex and he thus became an odd mixture of various styles, including ted, rocker, spiv and fetishist. Sid had also developed his own trademark look, albeit simpler and less variable. His thick spiky black hair was sodden with vaseline and sprinkled with talcum powder, while his heavy leather jacket was laden down with a variety of offensive weapons. Under the jacket his wiry frame was like a clothes stand, but his acquired strength from speed and drink was quite frightening. His tall stature (well over six feet) was complemented by his intimidating demeanour and belligerent attitude, which made him seem even taller. His look would sometimes be completed by a metal codpiece and then later a padlock and chain around his neck, for which there was no key. He invariably wore black jeans, which were occasionally adorned with a garter half-way up his thigh, outside the trouser leg. From time to time, Westwood would also drape Sex shop clothes on Sid, although he preferred the black leather and jeans look. Even so, the combined exposure of their clothes in this way meant that by the middle of 1976, Sex was the absolute bastion of punk fashion. The clothes were not cheap, but the gear was the very essence of punk.

As the Sex Pistols' notoriety grew, Sid's penchant for violence became feared and even celebrated. On 3 July he thrust himself directly into the spotlight with an incident at the 100 Club. The previously successful jazz cellar had now become the nucleus of punk activity and during the summer of 1976 the Sex Pistols were regulars. At one such gig, Nick Kent from the *NME* had come to see this new band. Kent noticed McLaren and Rotten pointing him out to Sid, who soon came over and deliberately kicked his shins, but pretended it was an accident. When the tall threatening figure of Sid stood directly in his way, Kent politely asked if he would mind moving to one side a little. Sid turned around ready to strike, but before he could act a friend of his had drawn a knife to Kent's throat. Sid quietly tapped his friend's shoulder and gestured to leave it to him. Sid then took out his faithful old rusty bike chain and thrashed Kent around the head several times, drawing streams of blood and cheers of support from some corners. Sid's chain was now a well-known weapon – he would often use it just to clear a space for himself on the dance floor, and he had only narrowly avoided being arrested for carrying it on the streets. The incident was obviously well publicised, considering the occupation of the victim, and as a result the Pistols were banned from the first major European punk festival in Mont de Marsan, south-west France. Despite the nature of the festival, and the fact that no single member of the band was involved in the incident, the promoters decided they had no time for the Sex Pistols, who they said were "going too far". Already Sid and the Sex Pistols were synonymous.

Sid, with mutilated doll and Nazi insignia: a curious mixture of innocence and shock-value provocation.

chapter 3

"Punks are carefree, and I mean completely... you know, like a football hooligan who kicks in someone's head and don't care a shit. The Pistols crowd are not punks, they're too vain."

Mark P. in Sniffin' Glue No. 3.

By September, punk had grown to such a degree that Ron Watts decided a festival was needed and so booked one at his club for the 20th and 21st of the month. The first night saw the undisputed leaders of the pack, the Sex Pistols (complete with a UK debut for Rotten's pair of bondage trousers), headline along with the Clash, Subway Sect and Siouxsie and the Banshees. This last band had been formed on the spur of the moment by Janet Susan Ballion, Steve Havoc, Marco Pirroni (from the band Chelsea) and Sid Vicious. The female singer christened herself Suzie Sioux (later changed to Siouxsie) and they clambered on stage to play, like so many punk bands inspired by the DIY attitude of the young movement. Sid was diabolical on drums and the rest of the band were equally awful. Their poor quality equipment didn't help – they had wanted to borrow the Clash's gear but when their Jewish manager Bernie Rhodes saw the swastikas that Siouxsie and Sid wore on their arm bands, he refused. These Nazi insignia were

The new Pistol: Sid on stage.

worn only because Sid knew it would offend people, that it was taboo, but he had no real idea of what it actually meant. Their terrible set lasted a painful twenty minutes and consisted of 'The Lord's Prayer', 'Twist and Shout' and 'Knocking on Heaven's Door', hardly an archetypal punk debut. In many ways, Sid was the most famous member of the band, but the performance was not about to increase this notoriety – after this sorry display he hung up his drumsticks for good.

Both Siouxsie and Sid were members of the so-called 'Bromley Contingent', a hardcore of Sex Pistols followers who tracked the band's every move. Other members included William Broad (aka Billy Idol), Steven Bailey (aka Steve Havoc/Severin), Sue Lucas (aka Catwoman), Debbie Wilson (aka Debbie Juvenile) and Tracy O'Keefe, who went on to become one of punk rock's first casualties and was buried with the word "Bollocks" written in red flowers on her coffin. Sid later denied that he was in the Bromley Contingent, probably preferring to distance himself from the group element, but he was clearly the band's leading follower. He later claimed he invented the pogo dance as a means of knocking the Contingent out of the way.

Sid's impact on the first night of the 100 Club Punk Festival was limited – his contribution to the second was somewhat more sizeable. With the Sex Pistols playing in Cardiff, the stage in Oxford Street was taken by Buzzcocks, the Vibrators, the Damned and French band the Stinky Toys. At some point during the Damned's set, Sid threw an empty glass at the stage, but his aim was wayward and it smashed on to a pillar, sending a shower of razor sharp glass shards on to a girl standing nearby. The girl, a friend of the Damned's Dave Vanian, was hit full in the face and went down with blood pouring from her face. The following week it was confirmed she had lost the sight in one eye.

Punk Rock Festival at the 100 Club, Oxford Street, London, in September 1976. During the sound-check, left to right: Viv Albertine, Sid Vicious, Siouxsie Sioux, Steve Havoc.

The police were called and Sid was arrested and thrown into the back of a van, where he was given a solid beating on the way to the Ashford Remand home. The following day, the tabloids launched into an anti-punk frenzy, denouncing this violent new form, and ironically bringing it to the attention of the masses for the first time. Although they were playing in Cardiff that night, the Sex Pistols were held fully responsible for the blinding of the girl and the press talked of Sid as "the fifth member of the band". Sid had a bad time in the remand centre and suffered violent nightmares – as with his strict schools as a child, he couldn't handle the institution and the enforced imprisonment only reinforced his views on personal freedom, a view encouraged by the Charles Manson book which Vivienne Westwood had sent him to read.

Despite over 1000 people attending the Punk Festival, 100 Club manager Watts announced that week that there would be no more punk gigs at his venue. Thanks largely to a speed-fuelled Sid Vicious, the Sex Pistols were now Public Enemy No. 1. Between now and Christmas, the Sex Pistols consolidated and reinforced this dubious but highly profitable position. While Sid had been honing his image and priding himself on his stature as No. 1 fan, McLaren had secured the band a record deal with EMI. With a £40,000 advance, one of the highest sums ever paid to an unknown band, and a contract drawn up in a day, the Sex Pistols were now ready to unleash their live mayhem on to vinyl. By the time the Sex Pistols broke the unwritten laws of television in December and swore at Bill Grundy on his *Today* programme, they were the country's most famous band. Their debut single 'Anarchy in the UK' was pipped to the post of punk's first single by four weeks by the Damned's 'New Rose', but the Pistols release had far greater impact.

After strikes at the pressing plant on account of the record's anti-patriotism, media bans, and then the Grundy incident, the Pistols found their debut tour in tatters with only three of the original nineteen dates still standing. At one of those they did manage to play, and much to their amusement, they found a priest preaching and praying in a nearby hall to fend off the evil spirits the Sex Pistols' very presence had created.

In the absence of any accommodating UK venues, the band headed for Holland, but got no further than Heathrow airport before the media had their fill again. Jones was sick and a couple of exchanges with the press took place, but it was a fairly innocuous incident. However, from the media reports the following day, it would have seemed the Pistols had ransacked

Sid with beer glass and customary padlock.

Daily Mirror

BRITAIN'S BIGGEST DAILY SALE

Thursday, December 2, 1976   No. 22,658

TV's Bil' Grundy in rock outrage

Sex P...

THE FILTH AND THE FURY!

E GROUP IN THE BIG TV RUMPUS
Rotten, leader of the Sex Pistols, opens a can of beer.
Last night their language made TV viewers froth.

When the air urned blue..

IEWER Bill Grundy ed the Sex Pistols ers with this comment: actually fail me the next guests on 's show."

roup sang a number — amazing interview got

Y : I am told you have £40,000 from a record . Doesn't that seem to opposed to an anti-stic way of life.

: The more the merrier.

Y : Really.

: Yea, yea.

: Tell me more then. F——ing spent it.

Y : You are serious ?

: Mmmm.

Y : Beethoven, Mozart.

: They're wonderful

: Are they ?

: Yes they really turn er do.

GRUNDY : Suppose they turn other people on ?
PISTOL : (in a whisper) : That's just their tough ?
GRUNDY : It's what ?
PISTOL : Nothing—a rude word. Next question.
GRUNDY : No, no. What was the rude word ?
PISTOL : S——
GRUNDY : Was it really ? Good heavens. What about you girls behind ? Are you married or just enjoying yourself ?
GIRL : I've always wanted to meet you.
GRUNDY : Did you really ? We'll meet afterwards, shall me ?
PISTOL : You dirty old man. You dirty old man.
GRUNDY : Go on, you've got a long time yet. You've got another five seconds. Say something outrageous.
PISTOL : You dirty sod. You dirty bastard.
GRUNDY : Go on. Again.
PISTOL : What ?
PISTOL : What a f——ing rotter.
GRUNDY : Well, that's it for to-night . . . I'll be seeing you soon. I hope I'm not seeing YOU again. Goodnight.

A POP group shocked millions of viewers last night with the filthiest language heard on British television.

The Sex Pistols, leaders of the new "punk rock" cult, hurled a string of four-letter obscenities at interviewer Bill Grundy on Thames TV's family teatime programme "Today".

The Thames switchboard was flooded with protests. Nearly 200 angry viewers telephoned the Mirror. One man was so furious that he kicked in the screen of his £380 colour TV.

Grundy was immediately carpeted by his boss and will apologise in tonight's programme.

Shocker

A Thames spokesman said : " Because the programme was live, we could not foresee the language which would be used. We apologise to all viewers."

The show, screened at peak children's viewing time, turned into a shocker when Grundy asked about £40,000 that the Sex Pistols received

from their record company.

One member of the group said : "F——ing spent it, didn't we ? "

Then when Grundy asked about people who preferred Beethoven, Mozart and Bach, another Sex Pistol remarked : "That's just their tough s——."

Later Grundy told the group : "Say something outrageous."

A punk rocker replied : "You dirty sod. You dirty bastard."

"Go on. Again," said Grundy.

"You dirty f——r."

"What ?"

Uproar as viewers jam phones

By STUART GREIG, MICHAEL McCARTHY and JOHN PEACOCK

"What a f——ing rotter.' As the Thames switchboard became jammed, viewers rang the Mirror to voice their complaints.

Lorry driver James Holmes, 47, was outraged that his eight-year-old son Lee heard the swearing . . . and kicked in the screen of his T.V.

"It blew up and I was knocked backwards," he said. "But I was so angry and disgusted with this filth that I took a swing with my boot.

"I can swear as well as anyone, but I don't want this sort of muck coming into my home at teatime."

Mr. Holmes, of Beechfield Walk, Waltham Abbey, Essex, added : "I am not a violent person, but I would like to have got hold of Grundy.

"He should be sacked for encouraging this sort of disgusting behaviour."

the airport and razed it to the ground. The press had found a fantastic tabloid whipping boy and they would not let up.

With Grundy suspended for two weeks for "sloppy journalism", the Pistols virtually redundant live and soon to be dropped by an embarrassed EMI, Sid found alternative means of entertainment – he formed his own band. Just as the Sex Pistols would mingle with the crowd before the gig, and then jump up on stage and start playing, so too did the audience watching them, Sid included. The DIY ethic that punk generated was perhaps one of its greatest legacies, and with this in mind, Sid cobbled together his very own punk rock group.

The Flowers of Romance were to be the most famous punk band who never were. Taking their name from an early Sex Pistols song, Flowers of Romance were an oddly balanced unit. Alongside Sid were Keith Levine, Steve Walsh and Viv Albertine on guitars, with Palm Olive on drums and a bassist just called Sarah. Sid took up vocals and made a striking front man. Formed out of boredom, the band had countless rehearsals in the Clash's studio and various squats around London, but never actually played a single gig or released any records.

Their music was loud and brash, not surprisingly very Ramones-influenced, and was distinguished by the drummer being arguably the first rock'n'roll stickswoman to use no cymbals. Sid attempted to pen some original songs, and amongst his masterpieces were the lilting 'Piece of Garbage', the heartfelt 'Brains on Vacation' and the slightly more accomplished but no less lyrically subtle 'Belsen was a Gas'. Sid even tried a stint, albeit unsuccessful, on saxophone. There were rumours that Sid was romantically involved with Viv Albertine but there is no evidence to suggest this was anything more than a casual affair. The band formed the same month as the Punk Festival at the 100 Club but despite their hard practice split up in February 1977. The split was actually caused by Sid being asked to join a band far more instrumental to punk's cause – the Sex Pistols.

Outraged press coverage of the controversial Bill Grundy incident, on 1 December 1976.

chapter 4

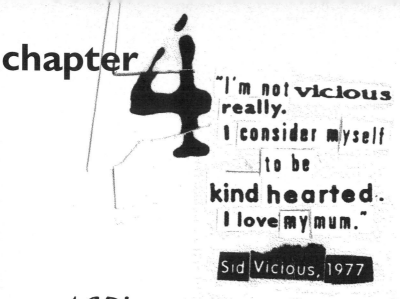

"I'm not **vicious** really.
I consider myself to be
kind hearted.
I love my mum."

Sid Vicious, 1977

1976 was a great success for the Sex Pistols but also a time of growing discontent within the band. Despite the initial discomfort caused by the arrival of Johnny Rotten, he settled in very quickly and assumed the mantle of band leader. Rotten was always naturally inclined towards Jones and Cook, the rougher of the three other members, whereas the suburban softness of the bassist Glen Matlock was never that appealing. Gradually his dislike for Matlock's tastes and way of life came to be a constant source of friction, until the situation became untenable. There had been plenty of public outbursts already – at the band's first 100 Club gig a drunken Johnny Rotten had, in between songs, openly taunted Matlock on stage and threatened to kill him. Away from actual gigs, in the press and during rehearsals, Rotten frequently ridiculed his supposed middle-class background and musical tastes. Matlock's father was a coach builder, his mother an accounts clerk with the Gas Board, and he had been brought up in a traditionally working-class London suburb called Kensal Rise. Despite this, to the other three, especially Rotten, Matlock was middle-class, and they hated him for it.

In addition to this, Matlock just didn't fit in with the band. He did not have the sneer of Rotten, the arrogance of Steve Jones nor the voracious appetite for the high life of Paul Cook. He was more sombre, more considered and thus an outsider. By the start of 1977 the situation had become impossible, so, despite the rising fame of the band, Matlock claims he decided to leave, although the band claimed he was sacked. His last gig was actually at El Paradiso in Amsterdam on 7 January 1977, but the press were not informed officially of the events until March.

Sid quickly becomes an integral member of the band.

In typical McLaren style, the undercurrent of personal friction was brushed under the carpet and a much more headline-friendly reason was given for the change of personnel – Matlock liked the Beatles. There was undoubtedly more to it than this, but McLaren's telegram press release in March was a comical blast: "Yes Glen Matlock was thrown out of the Sex Pistols because he went on too long about Paul McCartney stop EMI was enough stop the Beatles were too much stop Sid Vicious their best friend and always a member of the group but as yet unheard has been enlisted stop his best credentials is that he gave Nick Kent what he deserved many months ago at the 100 Club stop love and peace stop Malcolm McLaren."

Matlock has always said he left before he was pushed, and he explained his growing unease to the music press: "I've been getting a load of needle for ages and since the tour I knew it wouldn't last. It was mainly friction between me and Johnny. On stage he's great but he'd carry all that into the rehearsal studio and I couldn't handle it." He later told *Sounds*, "There was always a crisis situation in that band, John'd leave, Steve'd leave, Paul'd leave. I'd left twice before, so third time lucky." Either way, this left the Pistols with a large and hungry following but no bass player. Enter Sid Vicious.

The Pistols sign the contract with A&M Records outside Buckingham Palace, 10 March 1977, to publicise the release of their 'God Save the Queen' single. It was a spoof signing and the real contract had been signed at the A&M offices the previous day.

In fact, Sid was already turning up for rehearsals before Matlock was officially sacked, but Matlock was easy-going enough not to mind – indeed, he even offered to teach Sid the bass after he had left the group, but Sid never took him up on his offer. Sid auditioned on 11 February at the band's usual rehearsal room in Tin Pan Alley, Denmark Street. He was quite diabolical on the bass and so passed the audition with flying colours and accepted the position when it was formally offered a week later. From a musical point of view, it was a severe blow – Matlock had been the chief songwriter and easily the most proficient musician in the group. Of the 25 or so songs the Sex Pistols recorded, Matlock wrote many of them and recorded on over half. His replacement was a man who had learned the bass by playing along to a Ramones album all night whilst injecting speed, who chose the instrument because "it was loud and large" and who claimed "you just pick a chord, go twang and you've got music". However, Malcolm McLaren was quite open about Sid's musical limitations; as he told *Rolling Stone*, "When he joined the band he couldn't play guitar, but his craziness fitted into the structure of the band. He was the knight in shining armour with a giant fist."

Sid was perfect for the crisis in many ways. He was desperate to join – he had been painfully jealous of Rotten ever since the band had taken off and constantly pleaded with him to get him more involved. For Johnny Rotten, Sid offered an invaluable and loyal ally in a friction-ridden camp that was already splitting in two – Rotten felt isolated against Jones and Cook's chumminess and the manipulative McLaren. Likewise Sid was ideal for McLaren, who saw Sid's insecurity, his uncontrolled outbreaks and an apparent eagerness to try anything that was forbidden or frowned upon, as an ideal vehicle for his own sense of drama – here, surely, was a genuine pawn of destruction. McLaren later claimed he had been looking to incorporate Sid into the band ever since Westwood had pointed him out as a more promising figure than Rotten. Jones and Cook, although on a brief holiday when the final decision was made, accused Matlock of not pulling his weight and of letting his dislike of Rotten affect the band. When they were told of the split with Matlock on their return from their short break, they were more than happy to see him replaced. So the entire camp, for once, was in agreement – at the age of only 19, Sid Vicious was to become a Sex Pistol.

The irony is that in the aftermath of the split, the two people who stayed friendly were Matlock and Vicious. Matlock bumped into Sid in a pub shortly after he had left and Sid said, "What's all this about me and you not being friends anymore? We are, aren't we?" The two shared a drink and spent the evening exchanging friendly banter. The rest of the Sex Pistols were not so gracious – Rotten ridiculed Matlock in *Record Mirror* saying "He doesn't even play on 'God Save the Queen'. He's only saying things about us to promote his new band. We kicked him out. He was unbearable. Him and his snotty middle-class ideals." The band claimed Matlock's mother phoned them up one day and complained they were corrupting her beloved son. Steve Jones claimed he couldn't even play bass (clearly not true), and Matlock's face was blacked out of every Sex Pistols photo in McLaren's office. For his part, Matlock kept a relatively low profile until his new band, the ironically titled Rich Kids, complete with Midge Ure, Steve New and Rusty Egan, signed to EMI. Meanwhile Sid stayed clean of drugs and was practising very hard on the bass ready for his first gig. The Sex Pistols seemed back on track, or at least so it seemed.

On 22 January 1977, EMI released a statement which announced the termination of their contract with the Sex Pistols, despite the enormous success of their debut single 'Anarchy in the UK'. Their consternation at the band's riotous activities was strengthened when it became apparent that Matlock was on his way out – EMI A&R man John Darnley liked Matlock and felt he was the only genuine musician amongst them. When he asked McLaren about this and whether Vicious could musically handle the new post, he got an abruptly honest reply: "Well, Sid's never played bass before, and that's why he's perfect for the job."

Sid's first real duty for the band was to sign the new contract which took them to A&M Records – they collected a £50,000 advance with a further £100,000 to follow. The actual contract was signed the day earlier but a spoof signing was arranged for 10 March outside Buckingham Palace at 7 o'clock in the morning. A&M were a little surprised when the gangly figure of Sid Vicious turned up for the formal signing, as they had actually negotiated their contract on the basis of Matlock still being in the band. Sid didn't care what they thought – it was the start of his new job and he held nothing back.

Having been drinking until the small hours, the Sex Pistols were not ideally prepared for their royal rendezvous. On the way there Sid baited Paul Cook so much that a playful, but nevertheless violent, fight broke out in the back of their Daimler limousine, where Sid punched Cook heavily in between swigs from his bottle of Bacardi. On arrival, the band circled the Palace a couple of times throwing the V sign and pulling faces out of the window at the waiting press. The car stopped and they fell out on to the pavement whilst two heavies hastily erected a rickety old table for the signatures. When a policeman walked over and enquired what was happening, there seemed to be some potential for trouble, but Rotten threw a peace sign for the cameras and the tension diffused. Then a police van arrived, but the band had already finished and piled back into their limo which headed for an early morning press conference at the Apex Room at the Regent Palace Hotel in Piccadilly Circus.

Once inside the hotel, Sid swigged thirstily from a large bottle of vodka, and the press vainly tried to ask questions as the band belched loudly over their microphones. The only lucid member was Rotten, who made quite sure that all the tour dates were clearly mentioned. Meanwhile, Sid seemed not to care. The new boy was the focus of the media attention, this being the first time the press had openly been allowed access to him. He was more than up to the challenge. When A&M Managing Director Dave Green was about to respond to one question, Sid leaned over on one leg and let out a massive, foul-smelling fart. Then a woman from the *Daily Express* stood up and asked him something to which Sid replied, "Why are you asking me that dull fucking question? Anyway, didn't I see you at a party last week stuck on so-and-so's cock?" Not to be outdone by the apprentice, the rest of the Sex Pistols then opened fire on the unimpressed media pack with soda siphons.

Grabbing all the left-over booze they could, the band jumped back in the limo and headed for the A&M offices via Wessex Studios, where their forthcoming 'God Save the Queen' single was being mixed. They were now so drunk that a brutal fight broke out over who was the hardest member of the band. Sid's shoes were thrown out of the car window and his foot cut, Cook's nose was badly smashed and Rotten had a watch – recently given to him as a present by his mother – smashed. So by the time they arrived at the A&M offices they were paralytic and in an angry mood.

The idea had been to meet the people they were about to work with and to sketch out promotional plans for the single, both difficult things when various members of the band are unconscious. Instead, the Sex Pistols ran riot. Johnny Rotten drunkenly insulted everyone, whilst Steve Jones was found screwing an office girl in the toilets. Sid guzzled red wine then puked most of it back up on the carpet. He then stumbled into the ladies' toilet

Sid's first performance as a Sex Pistol, at the Screen on the Green, Islington, 4 April 1977.

to clean up his bloody foot and while in there he smashed a window with his elbow. His foot was cut quite badly and in his anger he smashed a toilet basin with his other boot. The blood was running freely from his wound so he stuck it in the toilet bowl next to him to soak the wound clean. He staggered out into the office again and passed out with a daffodil in his lap, only to be woken shortly after when someone threw a glass of red wine in his face.

Having pillaged the A&M offices, the band then headed for their Denmark Street rehearsal rooms, but not before the limo driver had refused to let them into his car, and demanded money for the damage they had caused. When they finally arrived, Sid collapsed on to a bed in front of a full television crew and gurgled, "I've had the greatest time of my life. This is my first day and as far as I am concerned it's great being in the Sex Pistols."

His first day was not over yet. Once he was revived, the band headed for the Speakeasy, a famous celebrity hang-out near Oxford Circus. Shortly after arriving Sid spotted ex-cop "Whispering" Bob Harris, the BBC Radio 1 presenter and host of the television show *The Old Grey Whistle Test*. Sid's friend Jah Wobble walked over to Harris and his four friends and asked when he was going to get the Sex Pistols to play on his show. When Harris said he wasn't Wobble allegedly pulled out a knife. A violent scuffle followed in which Harris received cuts to his back and his friend George Nicholson required fourteen stitches to a head wound at Charing Cross hospital, a deep laceration caused by Sid smashing a broken bottle over his head. There were also claims of a threat to Harris' life, which were taken seriously enough for him to move to a country retreat for a while. His solicitors were called in and action to sue the band started.

Bob Harris was a good friend of Derek Green who had only just signed the Sex Pistols to A&M. Harris himself was managed by the same man (Philip Roberge) who managed Rick Wakeman, who telegrammed Derek Green to say he wanted the Sex Pistols off the same label as him. Derek Green was appalled at the band's behaviour, not so much the wrecking of his offices but at the unprovoked personal violence. On top of the Harris incident there were also rumours of a second alleged attack on A&M staff, again at the Speakeasy. Green felt increasingly out of control of his latest charges, and so within a couple of days offered his resignation to Jerry Moss, the 'M' of A&M. Moss listened to what he had to say, asked him about the events of that week and replied "What you're really doing is asking us to choose between you and them. We know you. We trust you. Drop them."

With another parting cheque for the breach of contract in their bank account, the A&M affair took the Sex Pistols' total income from advances to £125,000 and won them the accolade of 'Young Businessmen of the Year' on the front cover of *Investors' Review* magazine. Even with the proposed 'God Save the Queen' single shelved, the band had still done rather well out of a week's drinking, screwing and fighting.

At a Glitterbest press conference.

chapter 5

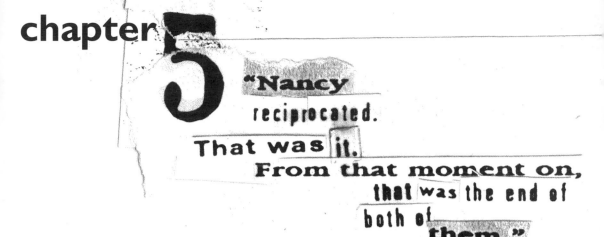

During this period of change for Sid, there was one other key factor that came into his life, and some say destroyed it – Nancy Spungen. She had arrived from New York with Johnny Thunders, whose Heartbreakers were due to join the Clash and the Damned on tour in the UK. A year younger than Sid, Nancy came from a very well-to-do Philadelphian family who lived in the ironically named town of Main Line (later the scene of the hugely successful *Thirtysomething* television show).

As the daughter of an affluent salesman she wanted for nothing, but she was a troubled child and very much the black sheep of the family. An unnaturally hyperactive childhood saw her undergoing intensive psychotherapy by the age of eleven for uncontrollable rages, and by her mid-teens she had tried to kill herself twice. Despite her unruly behaviour she succeeded in winning a place at the University of Colorado but she ran away from there and fled to New York when she was just 17. Her parents had only two reasons to be involved with her after this – when she wanted money and when she was buried. For such an unstable young girl, the move to New York was to have disastrous consequences. She took a job as a go-go dancer/stripper and within weeks she had ingratiated herself on the alternative rock circuit that centred around CBGB's and Max's Kansas City.

In a short space of time she had earned herself a seedy reputation as a desperate groupie and a shameless name-dropper. She loved to throw herself on to whoever was fashionable at the time, and there were claims she had brief affairs with Henry 'The Fonz' Winkler, Keith Richards, Richard Hell

Nancy and Sid, the happy couple.

and then Jerry Nolan from the New York Dolls. The toilet walls of CBGB's and Max's were covered in graffiti denouncing Nancy's reckless sexual promiscuity, and every act who visited the city knew of her in advance. To add to her repertoire of sleaze, by the end of her eighteenth year she was a heroin addict – she boasted of earning $100 a day as a stripper, all of which was funnelled into her main-line habit. When the Heartbreakers announced they were coming to the UK, she immediately joined the party, saying she was coming to England to get herself a Sex Pistol for a boyfriend. Johnny Thunders is widely credited with bringing heroin to the British punk scene; it was Nancy Spungen who brought it to Sid Vicious.

Shooting smack on the day of her arrival, Nancy declared to all who would listen that she wanted to fuck the famous Johnny Rotten (his close friends called him John, never Johnny). With her bleached hair, tough, squat figure and torn, tarty clothing she settled in easily in one of the many sordid squats in the King's Road. As promised, when she finally met Johnny Rotten, she made a blatant pass at him, but he was disgusted by her from the first and rejected her outright. Sid, however, was not so discerning. While everyone else picked on Nancy, Sid felt sorry for her and wanted to help her. Indeed, in his autobiography, Rotten thinks his refusal perhaps made Nancy more attractive to his witless friend: "Initially I thought of her as a filthy cunt, which of course appealed to Sid. To be hated, loathed and despised by me, he naturally went for her. She, being a woman of loose inclinations, reciprocated."

Nancy herself did not see the affair with Sid in entirely romantic terms either. Sid had once claimed to be "one of the most sexless monsters ever" and that "people were very unsexy" but hooking up with a sex-crazy Nancy soon changed all that. Rotten believed Sid was still a virgin when he and Nancy started seeing each other, and he certainly had had no serious girlfriends before her. That was not a situation that would last long.

Nancy later told *Sounds* how she seduced Sid: "We slept on the same bed for five nights before we screwed. We screwed as a joke really, he didn't appeal to me sexually. He said to me, 'How is it that the birds I fancy never like me?' So the next night when we were down at the Roxy and I said to him, 'Right tonight we'll screw.' And we went home and we did. We did it in the bedroom, we did it in the bathroom, we did it everywhere. On the first night we screwed, Sid and me, he had smelly feet and he wet the bed."

She also said, "I find him sexually attractive now. I've taught him everything he needs to know. I've put that sexual aura into Sid, he was pretty near virgin before. He was turned on by me like he never was before. He had a schoolboy crush on me." In the face of such sensitive and gentle seduc-

Sid had been injecting drugs long before he met Nancy.

tion, how could Sid resist? By the spring of 1977, they were inseparable. By the end of the year Nancy had irretrievably introduced two things into Sid's life – sex and heroin.

After the debacle of the A&M signing, Sid Vicious' first duty as a Sex Pistol was a sarcastic interview he carried out for DJ Rodney Bigenheimer of KRoq Radio in Los Angeles. He made an appearance at the Notre Dame

Johnny, a policeman, and Sid, in the Portobello Road, Notting Hill, May 1977.

Defiant pose: Sid and Steve enjoying the customary police attention, May 1977. No charges were brought against any of the Sex Pistols in this incident.

Church Halls on 21 March 1977, where the Sex Pistols were being filmed for NBC television, only five days after A&M had dropped them. The next day, Sid joined the rest of the Sex Pistols on a flight to Jersey, where McLaren wanted them to take a break from all the furore surrounding their terminated A&M contract. Sid was in fine form – at the airport customs, the outrageous-looking Pistols were easy prey for the rubber-gloved officers, but Sid was having none of it, as he told Alan Parker: "When we got there the customs bloke wanted to search my arse, so I farted in his face." The band were thrown off the island the next day.

Under guidance from McLaren, the Sex Pistols flew on to Berlin, with strict instructions to be photographed by the Berlin Wall, but once again Sid managed to scupper his plans by forgetting his passport and being stopped from going into East Berlin. He also got into scuffles with the German film crew. The band flew back to London on 28 March, and a week later it was time for Sid's first fully public appearance in the UK as a Sex Pistol – the date was 4 April and the place was the Screen on the Green in Islington, north London. The next day McLaren's search for a new contract for the band was rejected by five separate record companies.

Events started to take a more worrying turn just after the Islington gig – Sid was admitted to hospital suffering from hepatitis. He was regularly seeing Nancy by now, and his drug use had escalated dramatically, prompting the illness. To be fair to Nancy, Sid had been injecting drugs well before he met her, especially speed, and it wasn't even Nancy who first offered him heroin. His mother was a practising addict, so he had seen it before, although he had never been curious enough to try some. That all changed just before Nancy arrived, when Johnny Thunders waved a syringe in front of Sid's eyes and whispered, "Are you a boy or a man?", and his challenge was not ignored. Sid did not enjoy the drug that time, however, but Nancy encouraged him to try again and this time he was hooked. Now only a few months after meeting her, he was in hospital from drug excess. He even said of their fascination with drug use: "Sometimes we just injected cold water, just to get the buzz of seeing the blood and the needle going in. We had a needle fixation." While Sid was in hospital, Nancy was the only regular visitor, a factor which he did not forget and which cemented their increasingly close relationship.

Despite the absence of a record deal, the band were already recording their debut album, but Sid's bass playing was still below par to such an extent that Steve Jones had to play the majority of his lines. Sid's illness was a fortunate obstacle to his attending many of these sessions. When he did manage to attend, he played the lines poorly, after which Jones would overdub with a crisper version and keep Sid's efforts low in the mix. Sid knew he was substandard and his disappointment and frustration at that fact were drowned in bottles of vodka, which frequently left him unable to play at all. Before the split, Cook and Matlock had actually gelled into a very strong rhythm section, and Sid was never really able to compete with this.

Although the album sessions went well, the band were beginning to feel restless. They had made only three appearances this year, they had no record deal, and Sid was stumbling in his attempts to learn the bass. There was a very real danger that they could be overtaken by other punk acts. The Damned had followed their first ever punk single with what was probably punk's first album, *Damned Damned Damned*. The Clash were gaining substantial momentum with their eponymous debut album and a nation-wide tour in May 1977, and their more positive rebellion was winning many followers both in the general public and the music industry. The Stranglers and the Jam had both won lucrative record deals, while scores

Publicity photo for 'God Save the Queen', May 1977: Sid, flies agape, hides behind a plastic Union Jack flower.

Sex Pistols, subdued for once: summer 1977.

of other punk acts were lining up to shoot the Pistols off their pedestal. For their part, the Pistols had a drunken, drugged bassist who couldn't play and there were many whispers that Rotten was becoming too arrogant, too starry-eyed, too aloof. Their album couldn't be released without a record deal and the industry saw them as a dangerous proposition. Some said the Pistols were losing it.

The Pistols had the answer and it was a master-stroke. They signed to Richard Branson's Virgin Records, the exact antithesis of everything they stood for, with its hippy logo and beards-and-woolly-jumper outlook. Branson was looking for a high-profile band after sales of Mike Oldfield's phenomenal *Tubular Bells* had finally started to slow down. Along came the Sex Pistols. Branson chased an initially reluctant McLaren, but eventually persuaded him. The final deal was struck and signed in four days, with Sid autographing the papers three days later after his full discharge from hospital with his hepatitis cleared up. Rotten announced to the waiting press pack, "You thought you'd got rid of us but you haven't. The Sex Pistols are back." Virgin wanted to announce the signing with a seven-second television clip of the band in the commercial break of Bill Grundy's

Today programme, but Thames Television wouldn't allow the clip anywhere near the show.

McLaren booked the now infamous boat trip aboard a sight-seeing pleasure launch called the Queen Elizabeth, along the River Thames from London Bridge up to Hammersmith and then on to dock at Westminster Bridge. He packed the vessel with the band's inner circle, several journalists and cameramen, and loads of food and alcohol. Sid brought his mum and Nancy along, and drank heavily for the entire journey. Although the band mimed some numbers, as they floated past Westminster they played 'God Save the Queen' live, but Sid's bass work was drunken and shoddy. By then a minor scuffle had erupted between a cameraman and Jah Wobble, and the police were called by a nervous captain. The boat was escorted to the riverside by eight police vessels, and when its occupants were asked to dismount, more scuffles broke out involving baton-wielding police. In the ensuing fracas, McLaren, Westwood and eight others were arrested for a variety of offences. Ironically, both Sid and Nancy avoided arrest and slinked off via a hidden walkway back to their flat, where they eased their worries with yet more heroin.

Sid and Nancy were becoming increasingly concerned about the anti-Pistols feelings that were running high in the UK. The single 'God Save the Queen' was almost universally banned from radio and television, and many major chainstores, including Woolworths and W. H. Smith, refused to stock it. Tony Blackburn, admittedly never a bastion of alternative music, publicly denounced the record: "It is disgraceful and makes me ashamed of the pop world, but it is a fad that won't last." Derek Jewell in the *Sunday Times* myopically announced: "Punk will fade. Its apologists are ludicrous. There are ways to protest about the putrid faces of both pop and society without lapsing into barbarism. When it dies, it will not be mourned." The pressing plant refused to produce the vinyl at one stage. Mr Self Righteous himself, Cliff Richard, compered a meeting of Christians in Trafalgar Square railing against the evil band. Even the supposedly current publication *Sounds* altered the advert for the single so that the original record sleeve, designed by Jamie Reid, was not defacing the Queen.

Despite all this, the single was still the best-selling record of the week but was only denied a top spot by Gallup changing the rules for chart compilation – it is ironic that in the year when the Queen of the world's supposed finest democracy celebrated her Silver Jubilee, establishment forces contrived to render the music charts redundant.

Sid at the ill-fated boat party on the River Thames, June 1977.

But it was not these problems that concerned Sid and Nancy the most. Sid was constantly being hassled in the streets, and his name attracted countless violent challenges to his reputation. Their concerns for their physical safety proved totally justified the following week when a wave of attacks on the Sex Pistols and their colleagues brought home just how hated they were. Jamie Reid had his nose and leg broken, then five days later Rotten, producer Chris Thomas, and engineer Bill Price were attacked when leaving the Pegasus pub in Highbury by ten thugs with razors, who severed tendons in Rotten's hand. The next day Paul Cook was mugged by youths wielding iron bars at Shepherd's Bush tube station, and needed 15 stitches in the back of his head. Rotten was then attacked with a machete at Dingwalls in Camden, and later said that only his thick leather trousers had stopped his leg from being maimed.

Although Sid was not directly the victim of any attacks, the events frightened him and Nancy so much that they spent increasingly long periods holed up in their flat shooting heroin. Sid was especially vulnerable being dreadfully skinny, his physique wasted still further by the drugs which had reduced his already tiny waist to just 26 inches. When they did emerge into the outside world, they took cabs everywhere, fearing for their safety even on public transport. Sid was already living the life of a pop star outcast.

It was not just Sid's drug paranoia that made him feel this way. Rotten was justifiably terrified and phoned McLaren to suggest the band tour Europe for a few weeks to let the heat die down. McLaren agreed and so some dates in Scandinavia were quickly arranged. Before this tour began, Virgin rush-released the band's third single 'Pretty Vacant', on 2 July. It was also banned by W. H. Smith and Woolworths but still reached No. 6 behind Kenny Rogers' chart-topping 'Lucille'.

The week before Sid departed for Copenhagen, Nancy appeared in court charged with carrying an offensive weapon – a truncheon which she had in her bag – but fortunately the judge was unusually lenient when he heard of the recent attacks on the Sex Pistols. Although deportation was a distinct possibility, Nancy was allowed to remain in the UK after claiming that she and Sid intended to marry. The rest of the Sex Pistols entourage had hoped to see the back of her and were deeply disappointed. Sid was heavily into heroin by now, he and Nancy were fighting all the time and they were only quiet when stoned.

Their fears were allayed a little just prior to the tour when Sid announced that he was splitting from Nancy and fully intended to break his now

'I wanna destroy passers-by'; Pistols at large.

Sex Pistols posters.

Jamie Reid's famous design for 'Pretty Vacant'.

ravenous heroin habit. The delighted band flew out to Copenhagen, leaving behind an emotionally distraught Nancy. The split helped – Sid stayed clean, and played well, having improved his bass skills. The band were tight, relaxed and enthusiastic, and despite the eager crowd being noticeably younger than in the UK (generally 15- to 20-year-olds), some observers said these were the best shows the Sex Pistols ever played. Sid played well, concentrated hard and stood stock-still on the stage, occasionally curling the corner of his lip in a mock snarl. He was the picture of a cool, moody rock star.

The only blot on the horizon was Sid's impending trial back in the UK for illegal possession of a flick knife, an offence for which he had been on bail over a year. This related back to the September 1976 incident when the girl had been blinded by Sid's beer glass at the 100 Club Punk Festival. Although the police could not pin that particular offence on him, they tried to nail him on this other charge, which was serious enough to carry a possible jail term, particularly with Sid's already chequered history. Showing unusual restraint, Sid attended court in a black suit and tie, with his trademark spiky hair specially flattened for the occasion. Only a heavy pair of beetle-crusher shoes with thick rubber soles gave his true identity away.

Sid's mum turned up to support her son on the 250cc motorbike she used for her current courier job, and she parked it defiantly right outside the court. Sid had Clash members Paul Simonon and Mick Jones along with *Melody Maker* journalist Caroline Coon amongst those speaking in his defence. The case had taken so long to come to court because of a lack of sufficient evidence from the police, and even now they had no civilian witnesses and only one policeman speaking for the prosecution.

Sid Vicious

With each witness spending half an hour in the dock, it soon became apparent that there was actually very little evidence against Sid. His witnesses said he was on the other side of the club when the glass was thrown and that the police only picked Sid out of the crowd because of his reputation. Sid's lawyer said his career in the Sex Pistols could be disrupted or even ruined if he was given a custodial sentence and pleaded for leniency. To add to this, the judge seemed aware of who all the participants were and appeared sympathetic to the punk rock culture. As a result, and much to everyone's delight, he fined Sid only £125 and gave him a stern reprimand.

Sid celebrated by winning a bet that he couldn't go for tea at Harrod's restaurant with his suit still on. Later he reflected with slightly less gravity about his day in court: "I wore this really corny shirt my mum got me about five years ago. I must have looked a right stroppy cunt."

Just before this court appearance, Sid had nearly got married, but not to Nancy. The American singer Chrissie Hynde, of the Pretenders, was desperate to stay in the UK but her visa was running out, so she approached her friend Johnny Rotten about the possibility of an arranged marriage to enable her to acquire a green card for the UK. Rotten was unsure, partly agreed, then bottled out. Sid, however, was not so reluctant. He arranged to meet Hynde to discuss the matter, but when she saw the state he was in she refused. On top of that, the register office was shut for annual holidays and then Sid's trial was in court, so she never did become Mrs Vicious. Sid was disappointed, as he had asked for, and been promised, £2 to go through with it.

Once the trial was out of the way, Sid was free to resume his role in the Pistols, and returned to Sweden to complete the last few dates of that successful tour. On his return, he and Rotten argued angrily with McLaren about his proposed film project *Who Killed Bambi?*, a history of the Sex Pistols that the manager had already poured £50,000 of their money into to support the pre-production work. Otherwise the group were on fine form. The downside was that within hours of landing in London, Sid bumped into Nancy, made a hasty reconciliation and immediately started shooting heroin again.

At this stage Rotten and Sid were still getting on, but Rotten's intense dislike for Nancy, and Sid's apparent willingness to do anything she wanted, began to seriously erode their friendship. For now, however, he would often go out with Sid and just ignore the fact that Nancy was there.

On one such occasion, the three were walking along the street when a car slowed down and a horsey debutante leaned out of the window and invited them to her party at the rich man's haunt, Wedgies. Despite their being dressed in tatters, she thought the three punks were ideal freaks to show her guests, and they gladly went along and waltzed in. Rotten loved it and baited the rich and famous all night, scaring Prince Andrew and asking a disgusted David Frost for a dance. Nancy gobbled as much of the expensive buffet as she could, horrifying guests with her language and the piss stains all down her filthy jeans. Sid ate the food with his hands and got absolutely blasted at the free bar. Sid and Rotten were great friends again, but there was always the spectre of Nancy now, and that would never go away.

'Gimme a fix': Sid on stage.

chapter 6

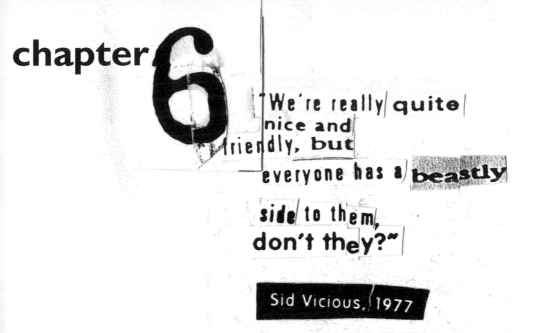

"We're really quite nice and friendly, but everyone has a beastly side to them, don't they?"

Sid Vicious, 1977

Unfortunately, England was still not as hospitable to the Sex Pistols as Scandinavia had been. Problems with booking gigs remained rife – a proposed show at the Rainbow theatre in London was cancelled after insurers objected and the GLC raised worries about the group's behaviour. Other similar rejections left the band with no choice – they had to embark on a secret tour, announcing the gigs the same day or the day before, and using a variety of pseudonyms, including SPOTS, Tax Exiles, Acne Rabble and the Hamsters. At the Winter Gardens in Penzance they were advertised as "A Mystery Band of International Repute" and over 400 people turned up for what proved to be the final night of a successful and relatively incident-free tour. Sid had been nervous about going out on the road again, but with Nancy by his side, a bag full of drugs and the secrecy that shrouded these shows, he felt a little more comfortable.

On his return, Sid and Nancy moved out of their Chelsea Cloisters flat and into a much nicer one in Maida Vale. Sid's health and lifestyle was now so poor that the lengthy seven-year lease on the new property prompted McLaren to laugh and say, "That's okay, he'll be dead by then anyway." While the two lovers stayed here their habits spiralled out of control. Nancy boasted of going to Piccadilly to solicit men to fund their drug dependency, and Sid encouraged, some say ordered, her to do this regularly. One time she and Sid were bored and looking out of their window, when Nancy spied a black mechanic working at the garage over the road. She duly went across

Sid shows off his muscles and that notorious cowboy shirt.

to him, gave him a blow job while Sid watched from the window above, and spent the £15 she earned on more heroin.

Sid was increasingly distancing himself from the rest of the band and the fears about his health were now very real. His weight was down again and he showed no ability to control his drug binges – heroin had become the single most important thing in his life, even above Nancy. By the time the band's fourth single 'Holiday in the Sun' was released in October, and despite the fact it was the first Sex Pistols record to carry the writing credit 'Rotten/Jones/Cook/Vicious' on the label, Sid was utterly corrupted by heroin. He was now living for the drug. He had been a Sex Pistol less than seven months.

Between October and Christmas 1977, the Sex Pistols enjoyed perhaps their biggest success to date when their debut album *Never Mind the Bollocks, Here's the Sex Pistols* entered the charts at No. 1 in November, thus belatedly reclaiming their mantle as punk's royalty. Conversely, Sid plumbed the depths, taking increasing amounts of heroin. While the law courts were debating the merits of the word 'bollocks' (finally deciding in the Sex Pistols' favour), Sid and Nancy were arrested on drugs offences on several occasions, although charges were never brought. This did not stop the tabloids spectacularly splashing the arrests across their front pages. The pair were now a magnet for police and trouble-makers alike, and they became increasingly entrenched in their drug-riddled flat. During the tour of record shops and radio stations to promote the chart topping album, Sid was frequently absent, often drunk and always stoned.

Life with Sid and Nancy was terrible. At the end of November, Sid turned up for a rehearsal that no one else attended and, after waiting around for hours, he gave up and went ballistic. He spent the rest of the day getting blind drunk, then returned to his room at the Bayswater Ambassador Hotel (where he was staying whilst moving house) where he phoned Steve Jones up and shouted abuse down the phone at him. There were rumours that he then tried to throw himself out of the third-floor window and that Nancy only saved him by grabbing his belt buckle at the last second. By the middle of the night he was paralytic, trashed the room and then smashed Nancy against the wall and beat her until she was nearly unconscious. His rampage was stopped when the police arrived after a barrage of complaints about the noise.

Sid claimed that he was then thrown out of the band by a despairing McLaren, who then asked him to rejoin once he had calmed down. Sid told

Steve, a banana, and Sid: 1977.

ANARCHY IN THE U.K. TOUR

SEX PISTOLS

FIRST MAJOR U.K. TOUR WITH SPECIAL GUESTS

THE DAMNED

JOHNNY THUNDER'S HEART BREAKERS

(Ex New York Dolls from USA)

THE CLASH

TOUR DATES

Tickets From

NORWICH University U.E.A
DERBY Kings Hall — Students Union, U.E.A
Kings Hall, Derby, Burton Stev
R.E. Cords, Derby, Nottingham Record Centre, L
NEWCASTLE Polytechnic
LEEDS Polytechnic Village Book
BOURNEMOUTH Village Bowl
MANCHESTER Electric Circus Lancaster University
LIVERPOOL Stadium Students Union, Leeds Poly
BRISTOL Colston Hall Hime & Addison, Manchester
CARDIFF Top Rank Students Union, Manchester
Virgin Records, Manchester
GLASGOW Apollo Students Union, Lancaster Uni
DUNDEE Caird Hall From Venue
SHEFFIELD City Hall Virgin Records
SOUTHEND Kursaal Top Rank, Cardiff
GUILFORD Civic Hall Colston Hall
BIRMINGHAM Town Hall Apollo, Glasgow
PLYMOUTH Woods Centre Caird Hall
TORQUAY 400 Ballroom Students Union, Teesside
LONDON Roxy Theatre City Hall
Harlesden City Hall, Wilson
Usual Agents

TOUR PRESENTED BY ENDALE ASSOC
IN ARRANGEMENT WITH MALCOL

SINGLES AVAILABLE

THE DAMNED NEW ROSE HELP (BUY 6)
available from even your dumbest dealer
PISTOLS ANARCHY IN THE U.K (EMI 2566)
from your cleverest

Nick Kent in the *NME*, "He just realised that my side of things had a point. That what I was doing was just living out that original idea of the band as four complete nutters going out and doing anything and everything. Just having fun, which I always reckoned was the whole thing about the Pistols from the very beginning." McLaren claims he said Sid could rejoin, as long as he stayed clean and away from "Nauseating Nancy".

Sid was a mess and his friends blamed Nancy. There were few people who openly admitted to liking her. Steve Jones hated her: "She was really horrible, she really fucked him up. Everybody in the band hated her. She was a leech, she took everything from him. She was just a groupie." Johnny Rotten called her "a titanic looking for an iceberg" and McLaren banned her whining nasal tones from rehearsals, the tour bus, hotels and gigs whenever he could. Chrissie Hynde, who had got Rotten and Sid work in the band's early days and remained a close friend, despised Nancy – she later admitted to cleaning her dirty finger-nails with Nancy's needle in the hope that it may damage Sid's girlfriend when she next injected.

For her part, Nancy repeatedly told Sid he was the star of the Sex Pistols and that without him they would disintegrate. She bragged about his bass playing skills and flying in the face of facts, claimed he was the musical heart of the band. In return, Sid worshipped her. Their relationship was a strange and violent one – she frequently beat him badly and fights were commonplace. At other times Sid would talk to Nancy like dirt and send her out to prostitute with men for drug money. She talked of New York and the rock'n'roll lifestyle of rock stars and Sid listened intently, fascinated. With his public profile in the band growing all the time, Sid was becoming obsessed with living up to his surname. Some said Nancy was on a slow suicide mission and she didn't want to go alone.

At first Rotten was desperate to help his ailing friend. He spent weeks trying to wean Sid off the drugs, locking him in a room and sitting outside, whilst Sid screamed abuse as the withdrawal symptoms wracked his frail body. But each time Rotten let him out, he would find Nancy and inject as soon as he could, and Nancy would be encouraging him all the time. He later revealed in his autobiography *Rotten: No Irish, No Blacks, No Dogs*, "Sid wanted to be hurt, that's what he wanted. That and attention. He'd get himself into all kinds of fights and he'd always lose. He was always covered in scars and black eyes. The sadomasochistic behaviour was something I'd never seen in him before Nancy."

Details of the December 1977 tour, before it was banned.

Sid on tour, in his hotel room

Sid Vicious

Johnny, Sid and Paul, backstage.

Sid the Pistol, with padlock and bare chest.

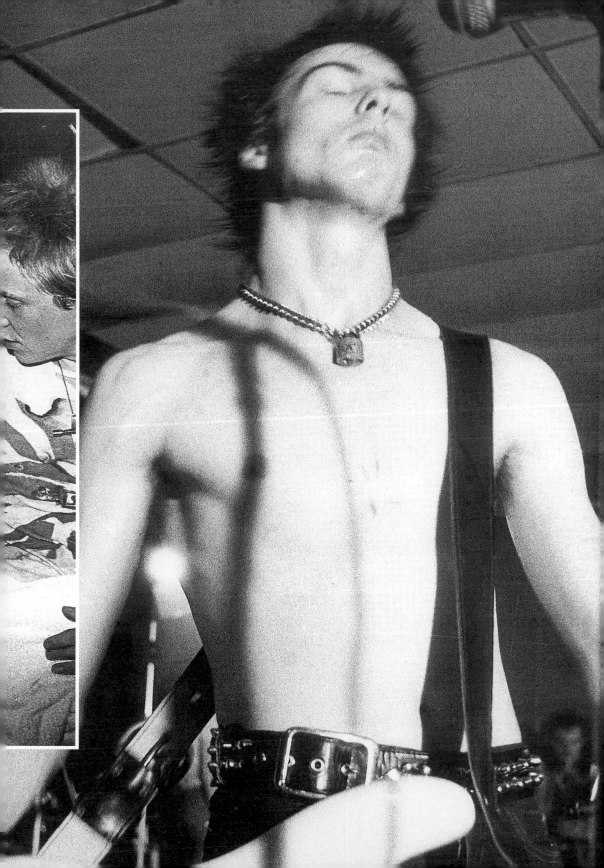

Steve (left), with tattooed fan (middle), and Sid.

Although he now blames himself for pushing Nancy on to Sid after he rejected her overtures, at the time he soon began to run out of patience. He was horrified by Sid's poor reaction to his fame once he joined the band and had thought he would handle it much better: "He didn't have the grasp of what it was all about. I thought he would fit and adapt. I didn't realise he was that stupid." Sid was much better being in the audience at a Sex Pistols gig. Being in the actual band was proving dangerous to his health.

The distaste for Nancy was so great that in December the band and McLaren decided to abduct her and send her back to America. McLaren feared that in the forthcoming tour of Holland, Sid would lose all control in Amsterdam and overdose, especially with Nancy by his side, so they hatched a plan to snatch her. On the first day they tried she never left Sid's side so it was impossible. So another date was chosen, when Sid would be at the dentist's and Nancy would be vulnerable. Sophie Richmond (McLaren's secretary at his management company, Glitterbest) offered Nancy a lift to the dentist to meet Sid but instead took her to Heathrow where they had a plane ticket waiting for her. When she realised what was happening, Nancy went mad – different versions of the outcome all have the same ending – Nancy escaped. Some say she ran out of the car at a red light and dashed into the Marble Arch Holiday Inn, screaming she was being kidnapped. Others relate how the car made it to the airport but Nancy caused such a noise when she was pinned against a wall that they had to let her go.

The Dutch tour arrived and Nancy was still with Sid. Ironically, Sid enjoyed the dates and claimed that the Eksit Club gig in Rotterdam was the finest he had ever seen the Sex Pistols play, and many observers agreed. Away from the gigs however, the touring party took it in turns to stay up with Sid to keep him away from the various city drug dealers, who all knew of his voracious appetite for heroin and smelt a handsome profit. Unfortunately, Sid started to lose it on stage at this point as well, and would spend many songs in the wrong key or even in the wrong song (a fact which belied his forthcoming 'Sixth Best Bassist Award' in the *NME*). Jones and Cook were especially unforgiving when he did this. The tension in the band was rising.

These Dutch dates were the first leg of a proposed jaunt through America and Europe, including a Christmas tour in the UK under their own name. By the time they arrived back home from Holland, however, four of the eight English gigs had already been cancelled and they had been refused

Rehearsing at Brunel University, December 1977.

visas for America because they filled in their application forms with their entire criminal records honestly recounted.

This monumental year, 1977, was to end in typically weird fashion with the Sex Pistols playing their last ever UK gig at a children's party on Christmas Day at Ivanhoe's in Huddersfield. The idea behind the gig had been a surprisingly charitable one – the town's firemen were on strike and a local factory had recently laid off many workers, plus there was a high ratio of one-parent families in the area, so the Pistols decided to perform for their kids in the day, then open the venue for the adults in the night. The band hired buses to pick the kids up, and when they arrived the children found 1000 bottles of pop, a huge cake and sweets for everyone. The party itself was a bizarre affair. A heroin-soaked Sid Vicious played with the rest of the Sex Pistols to 350 kids all under the age of fourteen. Sid always had a soft spot for children, so he insisted they play overtime, and even performed his own renditions of 'Chinese Rocks' (Johnny Thunders' anti-drug song) and 'Born to Lose'.

Ironically, Sid found himself quite uncomfortable with the kids, because he couldn't strip off his shirt, cut himself and sneer with any gravity – they just laughed at him like he was the party clown. The rest of the band were more relaxed, especially Rotten, who dived headfirst into the huge cake, after which a messy and hilarious food fight took place. The left-over turkey sandwiches were then handed out to the adults queueing for the evening's gig, which passed without incident. Afterwards, Sid and Nancy were filmed having sex. With the proposed Boxing Day gig at London's Lyceum being cancelled, the Sex Pistols' live career in the UK was over.

Sid goofing it up for the camera.

chapter 7

"If you give me the chance, I'll destroy America for you."

Johnny Rotten, Randy's Rodeo, San Antonio, January 1978

The Sex Pistols' American label Warner Bros quickly found out what they had let themselves in for, when they had to pay $1 million surety to obtain the band's necessary visas for the upcoming US tour. Even then, the delay incurred by having to reapply for visas meant that the northern half of the dates starting in Pittsburgh were already cancelled, so the band were faced with touring the less friendly south. Eventually, the authorities saw fit to overlook the band's criminal records and allow the Sex Pistols into America, amidst unsubstantiated rumours of alleged behind-the-scenes string pulling from Warner. Bans and venue refusals had reduced the original eleven dates to just seven, and with the exception of the last date at San Francisco's Winterland, these were redneck venues who were not used to seeing standard rock'n'roll, let alone the Sex Pistols. It was a deliberate guerrilla tactic cultivated by McLaren, that replicated the band's rejection of the established band circuit back in England. There were no Los Angeles or New York dates and they deliberately kept ticket prices low. There was even talk of McLaren allegedly encouraging the visa rejection, knowing this would eliminate the more conventional dates from the tour. It was typical, classic Sex Pistols.

If the environment that the Sex Pistols had crash-landed in at home had been stagnant, then the American scene was no better. They too were blighted with the supergroups and mega stars. The disco craze had been taken overground on a colossal scale with the smash hit success of *Saturday Night Fever*, starring a flexi-hipped John Travolta. Pomp rock like Queen vied with the adult rock of the Eagles, James Taylor and the sugary sweet

Sid on the US tour: the Americans had been primed to expect rabid punk animals.

Sid Vicious

Carpenters and Jacksons. Bands like Talking Heads and Patti Smith had brought some punk venom to the States but Uncle Sam had seen nothing like the Pistols. Even the Ramones were becoming cartoon imitations of themselves. Against this sterile musical backdrop, the country was suffering high unemployment and double-digit inflation, making it a nation polarised, unsettled and perhaps ripe for Sex Pistols success.

Viewing events in the UK from afar, the American media had not immediately warmed to punk rock. The *New York Times'* first piece on the movement only highlighted the violent edge, declaring "Britain's Latest Fad Leaves Trail of Violence in Wake" and taking a sarcastic, condescending tone throughout. *Never Mind the Bollocks* had been rush-released to prime the USA for punk's royal family, but it only managed to scrape into the bottom of the Billboard Top 100. One southern reporter claimed they broke hamsters in half on stage, and wondered if they would be dangerous enough in the flesh. Elsewhere, sceptical journalists joked that Sid didn't look very vicious. That's what they thought.

Sid and Johnny at the Kingfish Club, Baton Rouge, 9 January 1978: during the gig Sid asked female fans for sexual favours.

Rock 'n' roll star

Sid strolled through the 'Arrivals' door at the airport on 3 January 1978 with his usual sneer pulling up the corner of his mouth and his middle finger raised in abusive salute. On the flight itself all the band had been obnoxious, swearing and spitting at fellow passengers – one horrified lady scowled: "What the hell are we flying with – a load of animals?" Sid's last words to the press in London had been, "You can fuck off, we don't need the press, we don't need anybody." As soon as they came through customs they were met by Warner Bros representatives, anxious to keep hold of their $1 million, and fearful of the trouble that faced them during the Pistols' two-week temporary visas. The band met up with their American road crew, including two Vietnam veterans, and after a decoy tour bus led the press pack away (there were more press than fans) they headed for their first gig in Atlanta. On the way they were told by Noel Monk, their US tour manager, that there would be no hard drugs on the tour, to which the band laughed and Sid replied, "Fuck you, we're the radical Sex Pistols. Who are you, American man?"

Sid was in a bad state when he landed in the USA and the whole entourage knew the tour could fall apart at any minute because of him. McLaren was not due to join them for another three days, and the lack of a familiar manager saw Sid's restraint vanish altogether. The night before the Atlanta show, he and Rotten decided to go for a walk but were stopped by two policemen before they were out of the hotel grounds. Evidently their reputations had gone before them, and the local force were not prepared to unleash the unsavoury likes of Sid and Rotten on to their God-fearing community. After threatening to arrest them and laughing about what they would to do them at the police station, Sid and Rotten were ordered to return to their hotel. Sid was taken to his room and the tour party took it in turns sitting outside to make sure he didn't go out and get drugs before the show. At one point his minder, DW, talked to him in the toilets and Sid asked the war veteran and ex-biker for a fight. DW refused so Sid started to punch him hard, while his minder tried to keep his temper. After a while the punches started to hurt so DW grabbed Sid's hair and smashed his face on the sink several times, before letting the drunken punk slip to the floor in a bloody stupor. Sid spat out some blood, grinned stupidly and said, "Okay you're good enough, I like you. Now we can be friends."

First in the queue for the gig at Atlanta's Great Southeast Music Hall were vice squad officers from Memphis, Baton Rouge and San Antonio, the next three stops on the Pistols tour. Along with them were 600 paying public, five television crews and 30 photographers. The hall was not ideal for punk rock, and to make matters worse the band played terribly. Rotten sang flat, Jones was out of tune and their timing was awful. At one point, Sid took off his leather jacket to reveal his twig of a pasty white body, at which Rotten said, "See the fine upstanding young men Britain is chucking out these days." Most disappointing for the massed crowd was the fact that nothing more sinister happened than Rotten waving his familiar snotty handkerchief.

Sid was already suffering severe withdrawal and had taken to swigging heavily from a cheap bottle of potent peppermint schnapps, which was said to help the symptoms but only in large quantities. After the Atlanta gig he was desperate for a fix, but DW and Boogie (the Pistols UK tour manager) had been told not to let Sid out of their sight. Sid sought solace with a pint glass of vodka. Later on, however, Sid somehow managed to squirm his way out of the venue and ran off down a disused railway line before anyone could catch him. He had arranged a drug rendezvous and could not miss his chance to score. Sid went missing for the whole night and in the morning, when there was still no sign of him, the rest of the band had to fly on to Memphis without him. One of the crew, Glen Allison, was left behind to track him down, and the first thing he did was to ring around all the local hospitals. His search didn't take long.

Once he had escaped his minder's clutches, Sid had set out for a house where he had arranged to buy some heroin, but had got hopelessly lost in his drunken haze and taken hours to get there. When he finally arrived, he shouted at the supplier to get him his fix quickly and he shot it into his arm without delay – it was four days since his last score and he was desperate. With the syringe still in his arm, Sid then fell asleep. He woke up in the middle of the night and was bored and fidgety, so he took out a kitchen knife and carved the words "Gimme a fix" into his chest. His supplier host woke up and was horrified by the blood in his bathroom and took Sid straight down to the nearby Piedmont Hospital. It was thus that the wayward Pistol was delivered into the searching hands of Glen Allison. When Allison found Sid, he was barely conscious and stank.

The pair eventually got a bus to Memphis to meet up with the rest of the band, who were furious with Sid. Despite his physical state, the soundcheck was fantastic, but within hours there was chaos as Sid first attacked a security guard and then went missing again. When he was eventually located, he was in a hotel room high on drugs again and in no fit state to do that night's gig.

The severity of Sid's heroin addiction and the difficulties it posed for a touring band were finally beginning to dawn on the entourage. The Memphis gig was delayed for two hours as they tried to clean him up. By then the crowd were angry at the time wasted – indeed, some doors were broken down in their frustration to get in. Matters were made worse by too many tickets being sold. The original capacity of 900 seats had been sold out easily, but since then some seats had been removed to make more pogoing room. So by showtime, there were 200 angry people locked outside. Those inside had already had to wait over two hours longer for the band to show up. Prior to the gig, Memphis police officer Lt. Ronald Howell had said, "They can be nude, they can spit, they can even vomit, but there must be no lewd or indecent behaviour." Sid took to the stage out of his face on heroin. Backstage afterwards, Rotten shook his head in disdain at his bedraggled friend and sarcastically berated him as "Mr Drug".

During the day off before the next gig, the band took the opportunity to visit some topless bars and a Mexican restaurant – the tour food was ter-

Sid and Pistols on stage during the US tour: things were starting to go badly wrong.

rible and their daily allowance was only $15. Even though McLaren was not yet on the tour, his tight rein of control on the band's money was having detrimental effects on their morale. Noel Monk took the chance to meet with Warner executives and explain to them just how much of a drug problem they had to deal with. By now, Sid was not holding any of his food down, was dreadfully weak and only surviving between fixes by taking a mixture of Monk's own prescription valium and vast quantities of peppermint schnapps. It was rumoured that Monk had already taken to handcuffing himself to Sid, so that he couldn't possibly get away, a new game which Sid didn't seem to mind. Monk also informed Warner it was widely suspected that members of the FBI, CIA and British intelligence were now following the band around the country.

Thus far, the band's antics had been relatively low key, at least for the Sex Pistols, and the American media showed a muted disinterest in them. This was all to change, however, at the San Antonio show in the notoriously hard Randy's Rodeo, thanks largely to Sid Vicious. This cowboy bar, an old bowling alley, was reputedly one of the roughest watering holes in Texas and was packed to the rafters with over two thousand drinking cowboys and curious music fans. Sid (who had contracted crabs from an ugly groupie he screwed just before the show) walked on stage and shouted, "You cowboys are all faggots." He was followed on by Rotten, wearing an ill-fitting pair of bondage trousers and a famous Sex T-shirt depicting two homosexual cowboys standing next to each other with their enormous dicks protruding from their leather pants. Not surprisingly, the band's set was showered in missiles, with empty and full beer cans, bottles, coins, food and spit hitting the stage.

Sid taunted the crowd, spat at them and incited them to throw more things at him. After several minutes of this someone slung a full beer can at Sid and hit him full in the face, to which Sid replied, "That beer can hit me right in the mouth – it hurt, but I don't care." One man made his way to the front of the stage and started heckling Sid loudly, then decided to augment his abuse with a pie he had just bought. The pie splattered all over Sid's face, which was the last straw for him. He ripped off his bass, took hold of it by the head and swung it in a full arc over his shoulder and into the crowd where the man stood. Unfortunately he did not make a clean hit and actually smacked a Warner executive in the face. Watching this spectacle, Rotten calmly said, "Oh dear, Sidney seems to have dropped his guitar."

The man he was trying to hit started to climb up on to the stage to fight Sid, who was frothing at the mouth waiting for him. At that point, the sound cut out and the security guards dragged them both away, with Sid, covered in food and spit, shouting, "My guitar strap slipped." The gig was stopped for ten minutes. The pie thrower, Brian Falpin, later told the media as police led him away, "I don't like what they stand for; they are just sewer rats with guitars." The rest of the band were not to be left out – Steve Jones also swung his guitar at an audience member and Rotten blew his nose over the crowd several times. At last the Sex Pistols tour had erupted into the kind of incident people had waited for.

The extraordinary events at Randy's Rodeo were to have more serious repercussions for the band. For Sid, his ego swelled by a doting Nancy back home and an ever-increasing legion of fans, and his heroin habit perverting everyday events, this gig was all the proof that was needed to show that he was the only one living the lifestyle of a true Sex Pistol. He was the only one standing up for what the band had been supposed to represent in the first place. He was the only one who defended himself against the cowboys by hitting the man with his bass. He now felt his status as *the* Sex Pistol gave him a free rein to do what he liked, and to take as many drugs as he wanted. He was right in many ways – he was the only one doing all these things. In just over a year's time, he was also the only one to be dead.

By now the Sex Pistols had very much split into two camps of Rotten/Vicious and Cook/Jones, the latter of whom refused to travel on the coach anymore and so flew to each destination. This left Rotten looking after an increasingly incapable Vicious. During the all-night drive from San Antonio to Baton Rouge, Sid disappeared again, only to be found unconscious in the toilet cubicle, vomit encrusted on his face, leaning against the side of the bus. Before the gig, Sid reacted angrily to demands for him to soundcheck by saying, "I ain't doing no fucking soundcheck, I don't need no fucking soundcheck, I'm Sid Vicious." Instead he made do with a blow job from a groupie in the gents' toilets, crabs and all.

The gig that night was quiet compared to the mayhem of San Antonio, but there was still enough incident to make the headlines. The band were only average, and after Rotten asked the crowd to throw notes instead of coins, he picked up $30 from the stage. Sid was completely drugged up and oblivious to his surroundings. As a static and uninterested Pistols played on, he asked for sexual favours from the crowd and straight away a girl clambered on to the stage and started dancing with him. Since he did not stop her, she started French kissing him, and then slowly lowered herself to his crotch where she began unzipping his trousers, tugging at his pants to give him a blow job. Sid was only half aware, half playing his bass badly, but for the most part oblivious. He stood there like a child as a security guard escorted the girl offstage while another guard pulled Sid's trousers back up. After the show, Sid searched out the same girl and screwed her on the bar, while he swigged from his Schnapps bottle. He later told a bystander that "I wanna be like Iggy Pop and die before I'm 30." When the observer pointed out that Iggy was still alive and well, Sid just replied, "That's not the point." After this show, he was given the nickname "Fucking Useless" by the rest of the band.

By now Sid had lost control. His only forms of communication were sex or fighting. He was unreliable and totally dependent on a fix. He couldn't even be let out at gas stations for food. Instead, Monk had to bring the food to him while he was locked in the bus. He even had to be booked into different hotels at the last minute as he couldn't be trusted with the fans. The only thing he did right was to finally take a bath – the smell rising from his vomit-, spit-, piss- and beer- stained body was awful, and as he had not washed since arriving in America, it was with some relief that the road crew heard he had jumped in the tub.

When McLaren arrived in America three gigs into the tour, he realised to his horror that he had already lost control of the Sex Pistols. Cook and Jones were screwing everything that moved and drinking heavily. Rotten was ill and introverted, hating every second yet surrendering to the star treatment he was offered at the big hotels. Sid was out of his face and looking for drugs all the time and had taken to sporting a highly appropriate button badge saying "I'm a mess". McLaren, for once, was a largely helpless bystander as the events he had helped set in motion began to destroy his band. In fact, he seemed capable only of adding to the atmosphere of paranoia, by constantly telling the band about the secret services following them, the death threats and just how much everyone hated them.

Bob Gruen had been shadowing the band on the tour and taking candid snaps of their movements. He found Sid a peculiar but often quiet man and so asked him one day if he was okay. Sid replied he was having a great time and then said, "Do you want to see what I do when I'm happy?" He proceeded to cut a deep seven-inch gash in his left arm which immediately poured with blood. Gruen got Vicious to a hospital but they refused to treat him as he was so obnoxious to them, and so Sid just left the wound to fester. After a few days it was so infected and smelly that Gruen poured alcohol over it and sewed the cut up himself. Sid thanked him by holding a knife to his throat while he was asleep and only being stopped from using it by an observant roadie, whom he told, "I would have woke him up before I slit his throat." Sid satisfied himself by stealing Gruen's biker boots.

Pistols on the US tour: the clash of cultures was explosive.

The downward spiral grew faster. On the way to the Dallas Longhorn Ballroom, the bus stopped at a café and Sid was trusted with going outside. He strolled into a room full of about 50 truckers, walked over to the pretty waitress who was the apple of their eyes, and said, "Oi, cunt, I want food and I want it now!" After a near-death experience was only narrowly avoided by Monk's supreme diplomacy, Sid ate his meal, rushed to the toilets and vomited the food back all over the walls and floor. Later that journey, Sid spied some Hasidic Jews in their wide-brimmed hats, curly locks and long black coats, and was so impressed that it was all Rotten could do to convince him not to go out and buy his own. On their arrival at the venue, Rotten did his best to compete with Sid's obnoxious behaviour – as the bus pulled up, an enthusiastic fan thrust her autograph book at him for his signature. He spat at it angrily, only for the girl to run away, giggling with delight.

The gig itself was perhaps the worst on the tour. Sid was out of it. He was clearly blasted when he stumbled on stage and could hardly play a note, not even noticing that three of his four strings were broken. A punk girl who had driven all the way from San Francisco was dancing at the front of the stage and taunting Sid constantly. After a while she beckoned him over and as he leaned down to hear what she was saying she jumped up and smashed her head into his face, breaking his nose and sending a torrent of blood gushing down his chest from the gash she opened in it. Sid stumbled back and tried to carry on playing for a few seconds before spitting the mouthful of blood at her, and massaging the rest over his chest. Monk went to hit her but Sid stopped him. Sid ripped the pus-drenched bandage off the self-inflicted wound on his arm and threw it into the crowd, then licked his bloody lips and smiled at the punk girl, who responded by throwing him the middle-finger salute.

Sid stayed like this, letting his own blood run down him unchecked for nearly half an hour, all the time grinning in a "Look at me, I'm a star" way. When he noticed the blood had dried up from his nose, he walked over to his bass amp and took a bottle of beer from the stand, smashed the neck and dragged it across his chest, gauging cuts across it as he went. Rotten watched the spectacle in disgust and said, "Look at that, a living circus." Later on Sid got bored again and emptied a bottle of lager over his wounds while the band waited impatiently, with Rotten saying, "Whenever you're ready, Sidney." Sid carried on playing the set without realising that he had accidentally switched off his bass amp. Probably just as well, because by now his playing was atrocious.

After the show the rest of the band were furious with Sid's playing performance. Jones later said to *Rolling Stone*, "Sid was a tosser tonight – he didn't even know the key for 'Pretty Vacant'." Sid didn't care. He was too busy trying to persuade the security men to let him chase some groupies. He was seen at the side of the stage shouting, "I don't want to fuck them all, I just want to fuck one!" and, "I want to talk with the people, I just want to talk with the people." The security men spent most of the night guarding him and preventing him from driving away with the very same girl who had earlier broken his nose.

By now, Rotten was perfectly right – Sid was a living circus. As a bassist he was useless, as a friend he was lost, and as a human being he was slipping. Even with only two gigs and three days left, there were fears voiced that he would die before the end of the tour. Once again, on the way to the next gig, he got in trouble, with an incident that is now Pistols legend. Sid was eating in a truckers' café when a redneck with his wife and kids

Sid at the last Sex Pistols performance, at the Winterland, San Francisco, 14 January 1978.

recognised him, and felt impelled to challenge the famous punk's reputation. He walked over to Sid, made small talk and then stubbed his cigarette out on his own hand as an act of childish bravado. Sid laughed briefly, took his hunting knife out and slit his hand badly across the palm, let the blood drip onto his steak and carried on eating. The redneck and his family beat a hasty retreat out the door.

Outside the Pistols' next venue, the Tulsa Cains Ballroom, a Reverend Black was praying and holding a vigil, shouting that "Life is rotten without God's only begotten – Jesus!" Evidently Sid did not listen – he was highly strung and very aggressive all the time, swigging from his bottle (now Jack Daniels) and threatening any journalist who came near him. After the mediocre show, he pulled a glamorous blonde with a big chest and broad shoulders who was obviously not all she seemed. He made his move by saying, "Am I going to suck your cock or your cunt?" to which she said "cunt". Sid went with her despite her husky voice. He returned some hours later and described in detail the various scars and marks around the lady's crotch. Soon after he pulled another girl and shot heroin just before she started to give him a blow job on the bed. As the drug took hold, Sid's bowels emptied all over the girl on her knees in front of him, just as tour manager Monk entered the room. Monk, who had been on tour with the Rolling Stones and Van Halen and had stage-managed Woodstock, thought he had already seen it all, but even he couldn't help gagging at this.

With Cook and Jones ("the backing band", as Rotten now called them) flying ahead to San Francisco and the last date of the tour, Sid and John stopped off in Los Angeles to taste some of its famous night life. They went to the Whiskey, then the Roxy, where Sid jumped on stage uninvited for two songs with the band, but gave up soon after because "it was shit". The crew had now taken to waking Sid with a cattle prod which had been bought for the San Antonio gig after the band received various explicit death threats. Sid would merely receive the violent electric shock, open his eyes, grunt and get up.

And so the Sex Pistols arrived in San Francisco, hippy central. The mood in the camp worsened when Vicious and Rotten's hotel rooms were mis-booked and they ended up in grubby out-of-town accommodation whilst the rest of the band enjoyed plusher mid-town hotels. The day before the gig, they both attended a radio interview at Radio K-San following on from an expletive-packed interview that Cook and Jones had done the day before with the same DJ, Bonnie Simmons. Sid was largely incapable of conversation, but was kept in order like the child he had become with the promise of a new leather jacket if he behaved. Rotten was in a foul mood and the interview was a disaster. When the day of the gig arrived, the band were barely on speaking terms, but Rotten mustered enough energy to say beforehand, "Let's really fuck it up tonight. We'll fuck up these fucking hippies. We'll turn the tables, mates, and do something they haven't read about in

the music press." All Sid had to say was that he wouldn't go on if Rotten insisted on wearing his silly hats because "it feels like I'm backing Liberace".

Support was provided by local bands the Nuns and the Avengers, after McLaren's suggestion that any crowd member be allowed to get up onstage as support act was turned down by the promoter. During the first set, punks threw syringes at the band. The 5000-strong crowd was easily the biggest audience the Pistols had played in front of, and there were another 3000 turned away after the tickets sold out in less than a day.

True to Johnny Rotten's pre-gig words, the Sex Pistols did fuck up, but not how he had wanted. They were terrible. For once, Sid was not the only one pissed. After Rotten's opening volley of "Welcome to London", Sid opened with a few clumsy warm-up licks from the Ramones' catalogue including 'Blitzkrieg Bop'. It didn't get any better than that. The sound was distorted, and there was no bass or guitar in the mix. Sid was high and fell over five times. At one point, he needed a roadie to stand him still and place the bass back over his neck (by now, the spit was literally pouring off his guitar). Sid's only sizeable contribution to the show was when a can hit his head and he said, "Whoever hit me in the head – it didn't hurt a bit, so tough shit." The rest of the time he spent striking every clichéd rock star pose in the book (he had earlier been chastised by the band for copying Dee Dee Ramone and for not having his own style, but he had ignored them all). Apart from a three-song section towards the end of the set when the band finally got it together, it was a torrid gig. Even so, the crowd loved it and applauded everything that Sid and John did, including when they rowed onstage. When Rotten's legendary closing phrase "Ever get the feeling you've been cheated?" ended the gig, it also signalled the final breath of a band that had been dying for some months.

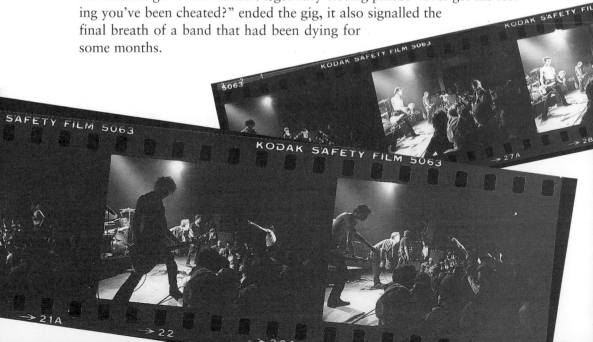

chapter 8

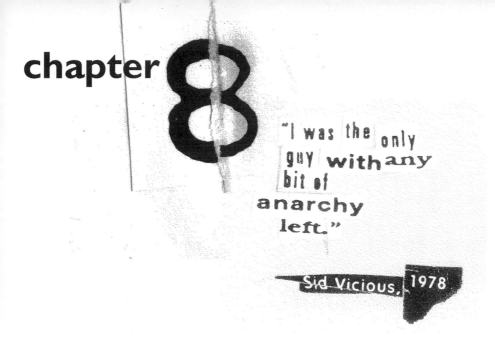

"I was the only guy with any bit of anarchy left."

Sid Vicious, 1978

After the shambles of the Winterland gig, the Sex Pistols finally imploded – people had warned that unless McLaren held a meeting before the tour to solidify matters, especially between him and Rotten, it would happen. Backstage at the Winterland everyone was depressed and McLaren said, "Fucking awful show wasn't it, they were just like any other rock band." There was an after-show party held at the Miyako hotel, but Sid was late and when he finally arrived at the entrance he didn't see that the plate glass double doors to the foyer were shut. He walked straight through them, lacerating himself badly.

At the party, Jones was seen dancing with Britt Ekland and having a great time, but Sid soon left and drove off towards Haight-Ashbury with a groupie for yet another night of excess. By this stage Monk considered the tour over and didn't care what Sid did – it was no longer his job. Sid was taken back to the groupie's apartment, where he shot some heroin and then trashed the flat, smashing her massive and prided record collection and reducing the hardened punk to tears in the process. He then took a further, massive dose of heroin and some reports alleged he was actually clinically dead for several minutes before being resuscitated by Boogie. Sid was then taken to a nearby acupuncturist, recommended by Winterland promoter Bill Graham, but was thrown out after he started to trash this house as

Nancy and Sid outside Marylebone Magistrates Court, 2 August 1978. They were becoming increasingly disenchanted with England, and less than four weeks later left for America.

well. He was then taken to hospital to be cleaned up, where Cook and Jones visited him briefly before going on to confront McLaren and Rotten and leave the Sex Pistols.

Reports of what exactly happened to precipitate the band split vary, but what seems certain is that in the next two days Cook and Jones approached Rotten and said they wanted out. Rotten tried to talk to them and said of Sid, "What about Useless?" to which came the reply, "He's your bloody mate, you sort him out." Rotten had grown apart from Sid ever since Nancy arrived, but now he was being held responsible for a man who wasn't even responsible for himself. He had had enough and later told Caroline Coon in *Melody Maker*, "I was bored stiff with Sid's juvenile behaviour. I was very anti-drugs from the start and I tried to help Sid for a year. But I've had enough of that social work rubbish."

One theory, which Rotten always vehemently denies, is that he became jealous of the attention Sid was attracting. When the Pistols had started, Rotten had been very much the centre of attention. He had genuine star quality: the stooping gait, the way he venomously rolled his rrr's in songs, his acid wit one-liners, his musical knowledge and sharp intelligence. Even when Sid joined, he did not initially compete with Rotten – standing still and thumping out the bass lines as he did, Sid was a perfect complement to Rotten's wandering, sarcastic presence. As Sid became more involved, however, he started to roam the stage and concentrated far less on his bass playing than on his stage activities. As Sid became more famous, his stage demeanour changed. While Rotten was the lyrical and vocal representation of punk, Sid became the visual attraction. As punk became more mainstream, Sid was seen by the tabloids as more media-friendly, more reckless. During the American tour, the crowds started gathering at Sid's side of the stage, either to bait him or adore him, but either way taking the spotlight off Rotten. The lead singer's unhappiness, coupled with the severe flu that he suffered from on the tour (as well as his memories of the beatings he had received in the UK), made him much more introverted. Sid became the public face of the band – he was the one confronting the audience most, he partied hardest afterwards, he was the punk they all came to see. On the other hand, Rotten was not prepared to act up to the preconceived packaged punk the American mainstream wanted to see. This went straight over Sid's head, and the more limelight he got the more problematic he became, which only fuelled his infamy even more. There was even a rumour that McLaren had considered sacking Rotten just before the US tour, to replace him with Sid on lead vocals. Once on the road, McLaren constantly encouraged Sid to be ever more outrageous, even applauding his self-mutilation by saying, "That's right Sidney, that's how to be a Sex Pistol, that's how you get to be a star!"

In addition, it was claimed that Rotten was jealous of Nancy, a suggestion which Rotten has also always loathed. Nancy clearly did take his best friend away from him, but by this stage Sid was such a shell of the friend he had once been that Rotten hardly noticed, and on one journey on the tour bus they had a furious row fuelled by their inability to get on together. Rotten especially hated Sid's arrogant claims to be a great songwriter – with the sick 'Belsen was a Gas' as his only major offering, it was a ludicrous suggestion. Sid's crude statements in interviews at the time clearly showed his escalating sense of self-importance: "I'm an intellectual, I'm a highly original thinker. Rotten's just jealous because I'm the real brains behind the Sex Pistols. They were so fucking useless they had to come to me because they couldn't think of anything by themselves." Sid also criticised all three other Pistols' tour habits: "The other three are real straights. I can't stand their lifestyle – sitting around in bars

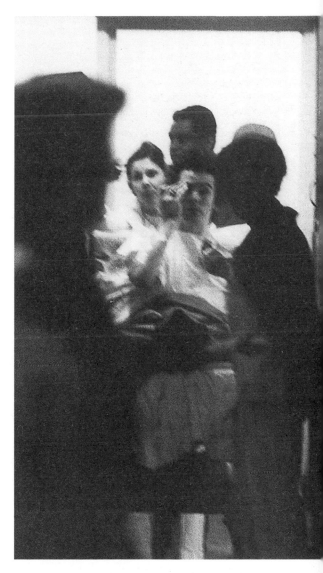

Sid being rushed into Jamaica Hospital in New York on 19 January 1978. He had overdosed on the flight over there from Los Angeles.

drinking beer, getting fat and screwing the occasional whore, it's disgusting." Other times Sid was more conciliatory, saying, "Half the time I just think I'm the most useless cunt in the whole group. I'm certainly the worst

101

Poster for the film.

musician. But I do believe that I'm the only one left with any real sense of what this band started out to be originally." Add this to Rotten's hatred for McLaren, the friction that split the band in two, along with Sid's wayward lifestyle, and it is a miracle that they made it through the twelve days.

As each day of the American tour passed, Sid convinced himself more and more that he was the only true Sex Pistol. He felt that the band were taking in many of the trappings of the supergroups they had originally hated, and in many ways he was right. The Winterland show had been their biggest ever, with thousands turned away. The stage was high and separated from the crowd, and an extravagant after-show party awaited them. Sid felt Rotten was enjoying the high life too much – he was being courted by the Warner's executives and apparently enjoying it all (Warner wanted Sid out of the group and felt Rotten was the only true star in the Sex Pistols). Sid laughed at Rotten and claimed his once close friend had bottled on the tour, and that he would never again be the performer he once was – he even compared Rotten to Led Zeppelin's Robert Plant. Sid had a particular image of the rampant Sex Pistols and was determined to stick to it, otherwise he felt they would just become what they had always hated. For Sid, this was the justification for all his antics, his anti-social behaviour and his attitude – he was determined to live the life McLaren had foisted upon him, determined to talk it as he walked it, and determined to deserve the name Vicious.

Rock 'n' roll star

In Sid Vicious, Malcolm McLaren was presented with a genuine rock-'n'roll freak. The problem was that the destructive free licence that Sid allowed himself was a key factor in destroying the very band that he so loved. Jones later told *NME*, "It was Sid who broke the band up – or at least, it was him who provided the straw that broke the camel's back on the American tour, 'cos of his habits. He thought he could do no wrong, be 'Jack the Lad', while all the time he was fucking up, playing different songs from us." When this was added to the redneck venues which McLaren had manipulated the tour around, the clash of cultures was explosive. The conservative nature of the southern states gigs aggravated not just Sid, but the whole band as well, adding to the general air of discontentment.

It is indicative of Sid's state of mind that while the Sex Pistols fell apart in acrimony and miscommunication, he remained blissfully unaware of the band's fate while he was shooting up with complete strangers. Cook and Jones flew to Rio soon after to start recording with the Great Train Robber Ronnie Biggs, and Rotten later flew to New York where he would change his name back to John Lydon, form a new band, Public Image Limited, and sue McLaren. Sid knew nothing of the split until he returned to the hotel after his latest binge.

Nancy and Sid: after the Pistols' break-up, they became even closer.

A confused Sid then phoned Johnny Rotten's hotel room and left a garbled answering machine message saying that he had left as well, but by then it was already over. The next day Sid travelled to Los Angeles and enjoyed his dubious notoriety for a few hours on Sunset Strip, and then took some bad drugs and was taken to a doctor who placed him on prescription methadone. Meanwhile, Boogie had been instructed by McLaren to clean Sid up and get him out to Paris where he was trying to start filming the Sex Pistols movie *The Great Rock'n'Roll Swindle*. Boogie was facing a hopeless task. Sid climbed on to his flight to New York already heavily doped up from his prescription dosage. Once on board, he swigged alcohol with his methadone and added some valium for good measure – by the

time the flight was half-way across America he had slumped into a drug-induced coma. On arrival in the Big Apple he was rushed straight into detox at Jamaica Hospital where he was treated for yet another overdose, all the time being allowed to keep his padlock-and-chain dog-collar around his neck. The doctor treating him issued the following statement to the waiting press: "Mr John Ritchie, a self-admitted prior narcotics addict, has recently been on an aborted methadone programme. On Thursday January 19th in Los Angeles, Mr Ritchie took 80 mgs of methadone prior to boarding a plane and sustained an overdose while in flight to New York.

Nancy and Sid in Paris, where filming took place for *The Great Rock 'n' Roll Swindle*.

He was brought to the Jamaica Hospital, admitted and has responded well to immediate treatment." He also added, with an abundance of optimism that revealed he had no idea what Sid was like, that "the patient is strongly urged to have follow-up medical care and long-range control of the narcotic problem".

Despite some minor flare-ups of bronchial complications from the drug use, Sid insisted on being discharged just two days later. He had effectively been abandoned by his former colleagues but was not down-hearted – he initially had plans to start his own new band, possibly rekindling the Flowers of Romance name. In defiant mood, he also announced that it was he who had decided to split the Sex Pistols up, despite the evidence to the contrary. He claimed the decision had actually come during a conversation between him and McLaren on a car ride heading for the airport where the ill-fated Rio trip was supposed

The 'My Way' sequence: a highlight of the film, with Sid singing, then opening fire on the audience.

to have begun (they missed their plane first time and had to wait days for the next available flight). Sid says he was ranting about being sick of the group and turned to McLaren and said he didn't even want to go to Rio, to which he claimed McLaren replied, "Why should we carry on then?"

Few people believed Sid's version of events, and in a sense it didn't matter. What counted was that the Sex Pistols had definitely broken up. The question was, could Sid find any stability now that his main *raison d'être* had gone?

Sid returned to London and met up with Nancy straight away to shoot heroin. A few weeks later Sid was seen in public to be out of his face when, at a gig by Johnny Thunders, he fell into the drum kit on stage.

Sid Vicious

Sid and Nancy were then persuaded by McLaren to fly to Paris at Easter to film scenes for the *Swindle* movie. McLaren had hoped to wrap this up fairly quickly, but he clearly had no idea of the severity of Sid's addiction, nor of the extent to which he was entrenched in his disastrous relationship with Nancy. Once they arrived, Nancy was in her element – she was in an expensive hotel with her rock star boyfriend, with the record company picking up the bill, allowing her to indulge in as many drugs as she wanted. For Sid it was also exciting, but for his general health it was not such good news. Recuperating drug addicts are encouraged to stay in familiar surroundings, but here Sid was in a totally new environment and had the city's greedy drug dealers sniffing around him all day. Furthermore, several members of the French film crew were junkies themselves. Even before filming started, Sid was smashing hotel rooms and acting violently.

Boogie, who had escorted him to Paris, was still hopeful that Sid would produce the goods, but was concerned about his lifestyle. He told *Melody Maker*, "I felt then he had a very strong talent, he could really turn it on. But ultimately I could see that Nancy ruled him. She had her drugs and I couldn't really do anything. They had these two bottles of methadone. It was very sordid." A deluded Sid fancied himself as a bit of a film star, but at the same time contradictorily denounced the medium with words that had a chilling irony for his own cartoon life: "I hate films. People have to act parts in them. Play people who they are not, do you know what I mean? And it's pretence, it's lies, it's just shit. It builds things up to be not what they are."

Predictably, progress with Sid's part in the film did not go well. The initial idea had been for him to record a new version of Edith Piaf's 'Non, je ne regrette rien' but Sid flatly refused to do so, saying he hated the song. For several weeks they debated what to do, all the time keeping the 60 extras and sizeable film crew on hold. At one point, a desperate McLaren even flew in Steve Jones to soft-talk Sid into starting, but it was all to no avail. Then, an executive from the Pistols' French record company suggested François Chanson's 'Comme d'habitude' as an alternative to the rejected Piaf song, better known by the Paul Anka translation 'My Way'. Sid was more amenable but still said the song meant nothing to him. Nancy persuaded him to do it on condition that they changed some of the lyrics. When McLaren and his crew accepted the new lines "I ducked the blows/I shot it up/and killed a cat", Sid finally agreed to start filming.

Even then there were disagreements on the song's production – Sid wanted a full-on Ramones pastiche, but the director, Julian Temple, wanted something more subtle. In the end, a compromise was reached where the first verse was done Temple's way with strings and a lush orchestration, leaving the remainder of the song to be thrashed out as Sid wanted. The final obstacle before recording could begin was Sid's relationship with McLaren, which was in tatters. Sid hated him, and demanded that he sign a piece of

Sid in *The Great Rock 'n' Roll Swindle.*

paper resigning as his manager before he started work. McLaren did so, but it is doubtful if the agreement was worth the paper it was written on.

Sid was now totally ingested in cartoon rock'n'roll mythology, fuelled by Nancy, and anyone who prevented him from living this life was detested – McLaren included. Even then, Sid refused to sing if McLaren was in the room. McLaren had a difficult time while shooting the film, as Sid's violent behaviour now perturbed him. On one particular day McLaren was furious with Sid's continued intransigence and made a room-to-room phone call to lambast him down the line. Sid gave the phone to Nancy and smashed his way through a side door into McLaren's room, which was next door, where the manager was still shouting on the phone. Sid stood there in only his biker boots and underpants, complete with a red swastika, and screamed, "You don't fucking talk to me like that", before launching at McLaren. A fight ensued and McLaren ended up running butt-naked down the corridor, before Sid cornered him in an elevator and beat him savagely.

Problems remained with the recording. Sid was so completely reliant on heroin that at times he was hardly capable of talking, let alone singing. Temple regularly had to wake Sid and Nancy up late for recording, and would often find them both with their heads down the toilet, nauseous from their latest fix. On one occasion Nancy turned round to him, face smeared in sick, and said, "That's what love is, throwing up in the same toilet bowl." On another occasion Nancy slit her wrists in such a way she knew she would be safe, but also knowing that Sid would not then be able to leave her for filming. Sid ordered drinks all day and would beat up the waiters if the wrong one was brought.

However, when the 'My Way' sequence was finally finished, it did provide one of the highlights of the film, with Sid singing the classic tune before opening fire on the bourgeois crowd he was playing to. It was to be a memorable visual epitaph, mocking one musical legend and at the same time creating another.

The Great Rock'n'Roll Swindle was a poisonous musical about conning the music business, dressed up as a history of the Sex Pistols. It was a gaudy mix of documentary, animation, drama and fantasy, all very episodic and incoherent. Sid's part in it was bizarre. He was seen riding his motorbike and singing "My Way", but, elsewhere, a scene depicting him screwing his mother was taken out. Apparently, Sid had not objected to this scene, but became very angry when they tried to get him to shoot up on film. Nude scenes of an underage Sue Catwoman were also cut, Rotten was seen only at gigs and in interviews, and Cook was entirely absent. After legal and financial difficulties, the film finally surfaced two years later to mixed reviews, by which time McLaren had denounced it and demanded his name be taken off the credits.

When filming finally finished, Sid and Nancy returned to Pindock Mews in Maida Vale and assumed a life of weird quasi-domesticity. They were now on a strict methadone programme but their daily dose was so high that they soon became utterly addicted to that as well, the withdrawal symptoms for which are worse than heroin. Their existence was totally drug-based. Sid was thoroughly demoralised and slowly coming to the painful realisation the Sex Pistols really were finished. He sought solace with his needle.

One positive development in this otherwise drab and seedy period was Sid's relationship with Glen Matlock. Despite the various media stories of rivalry between the two Sex Pistols bassists, they had stayed friends, so when Sid bumped into Glen in the Warrington pub in Maida Vale they gladly shared a drink. By the end of the night they had decided the best way to dispel these stories for good would be to form a band together, a group which would also help out with Sid's dwindling finances. Recruiting Rat Scabies from the Damned and Steve New on guitar, Sid and Glen called themselves the Vicious White Kids. It was one of punk's very first supergroups. Sid took vocal duties and, during rehearsals at the Eezee Hire warehouse in Islington, was impressed by Matlock's ability to play bass through an entire song. Just prior to one rehearsal, Matlock came back home to find Nancy sitting in his kitchen, eating a bowl of ice cream with her wrists slashed, saying, "Sid doesn't love me anymore." Matlock ignored her, picked up his gear and left for the studio.

While these rehearsals were on, Sid spied a gleaming new Fender Mustang bass in one corner, so he calmly picked it up, walked out of the courtyard and took it home. The band's first gig was at the Electric Ballroom the next day, but when they came to collect their gear from Eezee, the studio refused to hand it over until the Mustang bass was returned. Sid denied all knowledge of the theft and even Glen, who had seen him take it, was amazed at how convincing he was. Eventually Sid phoned Nancy and told her to put the bass in a cab straight away. The band then started loading the gear for the gig and, just as they drove off, the cab with the bass arrived. Matlock looked out of the back window at the studio manager taking the bass out of the black bin liner Nancy had sent it in. As he took it out, the black paint that she had daubed all over the guitar spilled out on to the pavement.

The Electric Ballroom had only just played host to two other ex-Pistols, as the previous week Cook and Jones had played with Phil Lynott in an ad hoc group called the Greedy Bastards. Observers joked that last week's show was the cocaine night and now it was time for the booze and smack night. The Vicious White Kids' gig that night went down well, even though it consisted of the same songs played three times, including 'C'mon Everybody', 'Stepping Stone', 'No Lip', 'I Wanna be Your Dog', 'Belsen was a Gas', 'Chatterbox', 'Tightpants' and 'My Way'.

Not surprisingly, the arrogant Nancy had fancied herself as a singer for some time and spent the entire gig on backing vocals, but the hideous nasal whine of her speech produced an even worse singing voice. Unknown to her, and thanks to quick thinking on Matlock's part, she performed the entire gig with her microphone switched off. Backstage, Keith Moon and Captain Sensible hung out with the band. There was even talk of Sid playing bass with Nico. Sid told one interviewer he needed to earn some money, so he was thinking of sending Nancy to America to have a birthmark removed from her buttocks, after which she could provide the household with a steady income as a stripper.

Performance by 'The Vicious White Kids' at the Electric Ballroom, London, August 1978. Left to right: Nancy; Rat Scabies (just visible on drums); Glen Matlock (bass); Steve New (guitar); Sid (vocals).

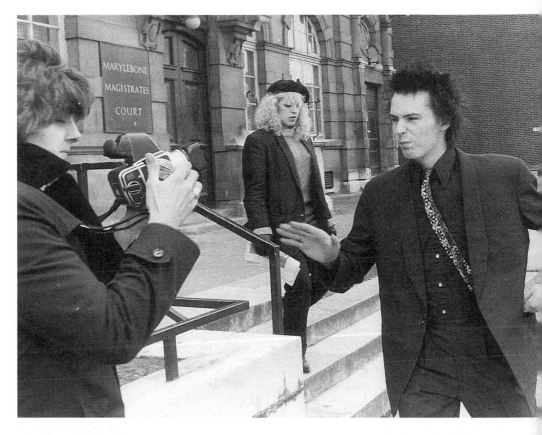

Sid remonstrates with photographers outside Marylebone Magistrates Court, 12 May 1978 (Nancy is behind him on steps). They had appeared on a drugs charge.

That summer Sid filmed a few more scenes for *Swindle*, including one with Eddie Tenpole Tudor fronting the band in a Johnny Rotten face mask, and he also recorded a version of Eddie Cochran's 'C'mon Everybody'. In June 1978 Virgin Records released the Sex Pistols' 'No One is Innocent – A Punk Prayer' backed with Sid's 'My Way', and such was the interest in the mutant band that it still reached No. 6 in the charts, despite featuring Ronnie Biggs on the lead track. In fine Sex Pistols tradition, a pompous and self-important Capital Radio banned the single, calling it "the glorification of evil".

As the summer of 1978 wore on, Sid and Nancy became increasingly disenchanted with England and began planning to live in New York. Their discontent was aggravated by two court appearances on drugs charges: on 12 May and 2 August they had appeared before Marylebone magistrates, charged with possession of methylamphetamine at a Bayswater hotel the previous November. Nancy had been filling Sid's head with tales of the decadence and rock star lifestyle they could experience in that screaming metropolis, and Sid found himself inextricably drawn there. The attraction of the Big Apple was increased by the poor lifestyle they experienced in

The night of Sid's 'farewell concert' at the Electric Ballroom, London, on 15 August 1978. Pictured backstage, left to right: Glen Matlock, Nancy, Sid, Steve New.

Britain – whenever he ventured out in public, Sid was getting into street fights and the intimidated lovers developed a siege mentality that left them cocooned in their flat, afraid of hostile attention from both the police and the general public.

Quite often the only places Sid could find some peace would be celebrity haunts, but then he would often incite trouble himself. He was still desperate to live up to his name and as he felt fame slipping from his grasp, he picked fights with a string of celebrities in London's music biz hangouts. During the summer, he scuffled with Paul Weller at a Jam gig, but Weller hit back by threatening him with a broken glass. Afterwards Sid screamed, "I'll get the little cunt next time, and I won't be alone." Sid also fought with Jimmy McCullough, but drew the wrong straw when he attacked a Marine who beat him up and left his right eye in such a state that he couldn't open it properly again. To make matters worse, Sid's drug binges had already taken away his once striking good looks. Despite being only twenty years old, Sid looked like a decrepit old man; he was deathly white and painfully thin, with a bloated abdomen and skeletal face.

In the summer of '78 Sid got back in touch with Johnny Rotten and they even considered getting a band together. Sid still had fond feelings for his old college chum, as he told *Flexipop*, "He was my friend. A really good guy. I liked that guy so much, I really admired him. He was so radical. I don't know whether he regarded me as his best friend, but I regarded him as mine." A meeting was arranged with the two on condition that Nancy did not attend. When Sid turned up very late with Nancy nevertheless in tow, Rotten refused to let them in to his Chelsea flat. Nancy was shouting that if they formed any band Sid had to be the frontman, while Sid screamed and kicked the door, but Rotten would not let them in. They went away for some drugs only to return in the middle of the night screaming to be let in once more. This time Rotten had had enough and so a friend of his opened the door and went at Sid with an axe whilst a furious Rotten wielded a sword. The axe missed Sid but hit Nancy on the head, and she had to be taken to hospital for two days to recover.

In the last week of August Sid filmed the kiosk sequence for the *Swindle* film (which was eventually cut) and then played a farewell gig at the Electric Ballroom billed as "Sid Sods Off". With their Maida Vale flat taken over by Billy Idol, they were ready to head for New York, but before they left there was one more disaster waiting to happen. They were doing drugs in their bedroom one night with nineteen-year-old studio assistant John Shepcock and fell asleep on the bed. When they woke up the next morning, it was some time before they realised that Shepcock was dead.

chapter

"You know people have said that I've grown up too fast. Well, maybe that's true, but I think I've grown up pretty damn smart."

Nancy Spungen, 1978

On 24 August 1978 Sid Vicious and Nancy Spungen set out for Heathrow airport to catch a flight to New York. Things had not gone well in the lead-up to the departure. First there was Shepcock's death, and then Vivienne Westwood phoned Sid to say goodbye and took the opportunity to tell him what she thought of Nancy. Sid had always had a soft spot for Vivienne, and so when she told him that Nancy had made him impossible to be around and that she preyed on his weaknesses he reacted by going home and beating Nancy senseless.

A farewell committee gathered to see them off at the airport, including Mick Jones from the Clash. Unfortunately, Sid's loyal mum was held up at work so that by the time she arrived they had already boarded the plane. Luckily, she managed to get a goodbye message through to them just before take-off. After landing in New York, they checked in to the mid-town Chelsea Hotel on West 23rd Street, a run-down drugs haven that was the first building in the city to have a preservation order slapped on it.

The Chelsea was rife with junkies, thieves, gangs and criminals of all kinds, as well as bohemian artists, poets and dossers. In previous years Dylan Thomas, Thomas Wolfe and Janis Joplin had all stayed there, but Sid had once again missed the boat – the hotel had long since been handed over to low-life. The first three floors were rampant with crime and regular tenants dared not venture on to those levels. Perhaps inevitably Sid and Nancy took a room, 100, on the first floor, after they had set fire to the mattress in their original room in a drug stupor. They had few belongings apart from Sid's gold records which were propped against the wall, and a

Sid and Nancy: they hoped to start afresh in New York, but everything got worse.

kitten he bought named Socks. The cost of the room was £15 a night, and they registered under the name of Mr and Mrs Ritchie.

The pair had come to New York for several reasons. They had had enough of England, of the police harassment, of the public violence towards Sid and of the oppressive attitudes. The dreams which Nancy had filled Sid's head with regarding New York were burning in his mind now, and he was desperate to see for himself. Nancy claimed she also wanted to be back closer to her family, although this was probably financially motivated. They were looking to start a new life, maybe break the drugs habit, start afresh, perhaps even get married.

Unfortunately, this was not remotely how it was to work out, and things deteriorated dramatically once they were booked in at the Chelsea. Far from breaking the bondage they felt in England, life in New York only increased it. Sid was well-known as an ex-Pistol and with that baggage came more of the same violence that he had faced back home. In a concerted effort to break the habit they both signed on at a methadone clinic, where Sid was attacked almost daily. With his weight down and his weak body under-nourished, he was taking regular and frightful beatings. With the Sex Pistols gone, Sid's fame was to be a fleeting affair, and the fascination the public showed with his life was now little more than a transient focus on his drug problem. The two lovers soon realised that Sid was not going to be accepted as a star, but as a punch bag to challenge in the street, or a good client for drugs. Their world began to fall apart.

Despite their differences in the past, McLaren had reportedly given the pair $10,000 to take to New York, so on the first night of their stay they got blasted in Max's Kansas City. The money was largely used for drugs and the pair's hopes of quashing the habit vanished within days of landing. They were buying heroin off the street and taking their prescription methadone as well; they were also gobbling an array of pills including Tuinols (barbiturates) and Dilaudid (a synthetic morphine given to cancer patients). As a result they were both constantly ill and very weak, Sid especially. Nancy was now suffering from a serious kidney complaint and her temper tantrums increased so much that she took to beating Sid, who was no longer strong enough to defend himself. Sid was not yet 21.

While in the Chelsea Hotel, Sid and Nancy conducted a dreadful interview for the *Dead on Arrival* punk documentary. In it Sid was virtually unconscious throughout, and Nancy had to answer most of the questions for him. All he could manage was a few barely audible and largely meaningless ramblings, while his girlfriend tried to stop him stubbing his cigarette out on her, avoided his vomit and kept him awake. It was a sordid and pitiful sight. This famous interview was one of several they did during this period, but as time passed they became less of a media draw. They would ask for money or drugs for interviews and when refused become violent. Not long after, Sid and Nancy visited her family for a week which her parents recall as a total nightmare.

McLaren's money would not last forever, and at the rate they were getting through drugs Sid and Nancy knew they had to find more cash. With Nancy as Sid's self-appointed manager, she booked him some gigs at the Max's Kansas City venue in Manhattan, which was part of the same circuit as CBGB's. Sid performed several times in September with a variety of punk celebrities, including the Clash's Mick Jones, and Johnny Thunders and Jerry Nolan from the New York Dolls. One of these gigs was taped and Virgin Records later released it, a record which shows what a state Sid was now in. As he sang 'My Way' he bastardised the entire song to "I killed the cat" because he had forgotten the words. The set was brief and poor, with Sid barely being able to stand up some nights. Among the tracks included were 'Search and Destroy', 'I Wanna be Your Dog' and 'Belsen was a Gas'. People who came to see a vibrant ex-Sex Pistol found themselves embarrassed by a young man just out of his teens, looking like a pensioner, and merely going through the dreadful motions. At every gig Nancy was obnoxious to the press that bothered to attend and ungrateful to those who helped out at each show. By the start of October they were totally isolated and depressed. Sid missed London and wanted to return home, vowing to go back after just one more show on Halloween night in Philadelphia. Sid never made it back to the UK.

"Listen kid, why'd you do that?"
"Why did I do what?"
"Why'd you kill the girl?"
"I didn't kill her."
"If you didn't kill her, why can't you look me straight in the face?"
"OK mate, I'm looking you straight in the face. I didn't kill her!"

The policeman laughed at the denial, slammed Sid Vicious against the wall and handcuffed him. Nearby, under the bathroom sink lay the blood-soaked body of Nancy Spungen. Contrasting reports claimed Sid told the police to shoot him because "his baby was dead", whilst others said he shouted, "You can't arrest me, I'm a rock'n'roll star." But Sid was arrested and taken outside, kicking and screaming obscenities all the way into the waiting police car, which took him to the fearful Rikers Island prison on remand. Sid and Nancy's joint spiral of destruction had finally come to a close.

Sid Vicious

As with many such incidents, the actual events will never be known for certain and there are many conflicting reports about what happened that night. In among the idle gossip and factual debris, there are some snippets that suggest likely causes and events.

Fact One is that during the day before the murder, 12 October, Sid, Nancy, Stiv Bators from the Dead Boys and Neon Leon, a sometime punk and drug addict they had befriended in the Chelsea, were shopping in New York. On their trip they spent some time in a knife shop in Times Square. Sid was tired of being beaten when he went out and had decided to protect himself with something more than just his fists. One of the biggest sources of trouble was the Chelsea itself, whose manager turned a blind eye to the underworld activity going on in there. So Sid bought a folding hunting knife, with a carving of a black jaguar on the handle.

Fact Two: what is also clear is that by 5 a.m. the following morning, Nancy lay dead in room 100, blood pouring from a one-inch laceration in

Nancy's body is carried from the Chelsea Hotel on 12 October 1978. She had been stabbed to death.

Sid outside the court room.

her abdomen made by that same hunting knife. The cut itself may not have been that serious, but Nancy failed to staunch the flow of blood, added to which her drug-riddled internal organs had been rendered so weak by her lifestyle that she simply did not have the strength to hold on. She was wearing just her black knickers and matching bra. From the blood stains throughout the room, it appeared she had lain in bed for some time before dragging herself across to the bathroom, looking at herself in the mirror, and then slumping on to the floor, where the unchecked internal haemorrhaging killed her. Just what happened between these two facts is unclear.

The obvious theory was that Sid had killed Nancy. They had always fought. Only that week, Sid had hit her with his guitar, and tenants also claimed he had chased her around the hotel and dangled her out of a seventh-floor window after another argument. On the night in question, they had been desperate for drugs, so Sid had wandered around the hotel looking for a supply. A black bellhop had caught the wrong end of Sid's venom when the ex-Pistol hurled racist abuse at him, and the bellhop responded by punching Sid's nose, breaking it in the process. Sid had returned to the room in a rage, whereupon Nancy had nagged him and ridiculed him for not bringing any drugs back, finally hitting him on the same spot he had just been punched. Sid flew into a rage and during the course of the argument he had stabbed her in the stomach. The two were drugged and, as with most of their arguments, they were quickly reconciled. Not realising the extent of the damage inflicted on Nancy, they climbed in bed in each other's arms and slipped into a deep sleep. Sid recalled waking up in the middle of the night and seeing Nancy fingering his hunting knife, but he was too drugged to react and rapidly fell back to sleep. When he woke the next morning, he saw "blood everywhere, on the sheets, on the pillow case, all over the mattress and on the floor leading to the bathroom. My first thought was that she had been killed." Then he found Nancy under the sink, dead. After futile attempts to revive her, he ran out in to the lobby and shouted for help before calling reception and saying, "Get an ambulance up here quick, I'm not kidding!" Five minutes later and it was not the ambulance but the police who arrived. They found Sid Vicious on the edge of his bed, speechless and in shock, with what turned out to be enough Tuinol (nine doses) in his body to kill a horse. The nearby body of his heroin-addict girlfriend Nancy had suffered a wound apparently caused by Sid's very own knife. The connection was only too obvious. By the time Sid had been taken to the Third Homicide division on 51st Street, he had allegedly said, "I did it because I'm a dirty dog."

Another theory was that the death had been the result of a botched suicide attempt. Nancy and Sid had talked of this for many months, and it was a long-standing joke amongst punk's inner circle. Since their arrival in New York and the deterioration in their mental and physical health, people had become genuinely concerned that these idle threats were edging ever closer to reality. They were both deeply depressed the week before the murder and talked openly of impending suicide. Nancy reportedly needed an operation for a failing kidney and her family had disowned her after their latest visit.

As an indication of just how bad a state Nancy was in, police pathologists noted she started to decompose after only seven hours – even elderly people usually take 48 hours. Sid's health was much the same as hers had been. He complained he didn't look so good as he once had, and he even gave his gold records and beloved leather jacket to Neon Leon (Leon disappeared for a few days after the killing, and his account of the night's events clashed with other witnesses, leading to allegations that he may have stolen the belongings). Perhaps this was meant to be Sid's last act of generosity before he and Nancy died. Perhaps Sid stabbed Nancy, then tried to overdose but miscalculated. Alternatively, maybe Sid overdosed, leaving Nancy to stab herself as her half of the bargain.

Certainly when the punk community heard of the death, their immediate reaction was that it must have been a botched suicide attempt. Rumours suggested that Sid told police as much when they arrested him and claimed they had been planning it for weeks. Possibly. The questions remain, however – why didn't Nancy overdose as well? Why choose such a painful and lengthy method of dying?

Another theory was that a third party was involved. One suggestion was that a Puerto Rican drugs gang had killed Nancy after she had argued with them earlier in the day. The involvement of someone else was given more weight when the police revealed that a substantial amount of cash had been stolen from room 100 during the night. Then *Rolling Stone* magazine unearthed a witness to another possible murder suspect. Rockets Redglarc, a sometime punk and hairdresser with a drug habit, claimed to have been with the couple until 5 a.m. the morning Nancy was discovered – he had known them for a month and occasionally supplied them with Dilaudid. He claimed Nancy called him up at 1.30 a.m. and asked for 40 pills, which he didn't have, but instead he went to see her with a much smaller amount anyway. He left them safe and well in their room and went downstairs to make a phone call in the hotel lobby. He alleged he had seen a local drug dealer known as Steve, who had a history of mental illness, heading towards room 100. This sounded feasible, but there were also yet more unsubstantiated stories of unnamed thieves killing Nancy. The third party theory was possible, but which third party?

There were conflicting reports about all elements of the murder. An exact time of death was never pin-pointed. It was unclear who called the police, whether there was a third party involved, and what motives were involved. Although the city police classed Sid as the prime suspect and charged him with second degree murder, by the time Nancy's body was taken out in a green body bag at 5.20 p.m., there was already some doubt as to whether he had actually done it.

The media response to these admittedly dramatic events was frenzied. The British tabloids splashed the story across their front pages, and there were wildly erratic reports about the murder. Some said Sid was found wandering the New York Streets in a drugged daze asking, "Where's Nancy?" Others alleged Nancy's was a well-known face on the New York S&M scene and that there may be a perverted connection there. No major editorials appeared, just titillating minor features. The only lengthy piece in the non-music press appeared a week later when Anthony Burgess, the acclaimed writer of many classic novels including *Clockwork Orange*, published a ludicrous essay entitled "Why punk had to end in evil", in which he drew together such sources as Pope John Paul II and Jane Austen. Equally ridiculous but less critically acclaimed was a tabloid piece written by a clairvoyant claiming to have reached Nancy on the other side. To be fair, Sid had hardly helped himself in winning the media over – one frustrated writer had ridiculed his drugged state and useless interview ability just before he left for New York by saying, "Ah, Sid's eyes are open, let's leap in quick."

In the US the response was more protracted but even less sympathetic. The broadsheet media had never given Sid or the Sex Pistols any credence whatsoever, so they viewed this latest sordid little chapter as only to be expected. Sid had long been lined up for the rock'n'roll mortuary and the only surprise was that Nancy went first. They talked of his penchant for self-mutilation, his drug abuse and his abusive nature, most damagingly so in the New York Post. All presumption of innocence was lost in a flurry of speculative stories – one television station even broadcast a parent-scaring feature called "Will Your Son Turn into Sid Vicious?"

Within days "Sid Is Innocent" badges started to appear in London, and even Westwood and McLaren got in on the act. A T-shirt was put on sale in their shop (now called Seditionaries) with a picture of Sid surrounded by roses saying, "She's dead, I'm alive, I'm yours". For some this was taking McLaren's "cash from chaos" ethos too far, but he and Westwood had never made a secret of their intense dislike of Nancy. Warner Brothers were less happy to be involved, and within days had dropped Sid and the remaining two Sex Pistols, Cook and Jones, from their American contracts. Johnny Rotten was pestered for quotes about Nancy's death, but he simply said, "I don't see why I should have any feelings about it at all." All that was left was for Johnny Thunders to say of Sid's arrest, "Well, he beat Keith Richards for the story of the year."

On 13 October 1978 Sid appeared at a hearing in a New York courtroom where he was formally charged with second degree murder, under his real name of John Simon Ritchie, and remanded for reports at Rikers Island. He appeared highly distressed and still out of it on drugs. The minimum sentence if found guilty was seven years – the maximum was 25. Much to the anger of the police, Sid was granted bail, set at $25,000, although as no one was present to offer the money he was sent to the island jail's detoxification wing, where he spent four

Sid after leaving prison.

Sid out on bail, with Johnny Thunders at the Palladium, late 1978.

miserable days. The police were furious and there was even an unsubstantiated rumour that the bail had been granted by illegal behind-the-doors manoeuvres. After all, Sid was an alien, and an unemployed, known-violent criminal.

Rikers Island is a heavily guarded remand centre and short-term jail located in the middle of the Hudson River, near the airport. In 1978 the prison population consisted mostly of blacks and Puerto Ricans. The prison was notoriously violent, and sexual abuse amongst inmates was rife, as was hard drug use. Into this violent cauldron came Sid Vicious, a white Englishman aged 20, who they had all seen on television, and who appeared to think he was special. There could not have been an easier and more appealing target sent to the jail for years. Sid suffered abuse and nightmares in the four days he spent there, but never openly spoke about this. He later revealed that he had written some songs during his brief incarceration, but these never surfaced.

Sid's mother arrived in New York with her sleeping bag on the Sunday

Sid's bail is confirmed on 21 November.

and visited her son immediately in the prison's hospital wing. While she was there an angry Sid told her, "Listen, I'm not a mummy's boy, I'll fight my own battles." Sid also angrily denied to an *NME* journalist that he had ever confessed to Nancy's murder and stated he would most definitely be pleading "not guilty". He seemed unaware that the police department considered this an open-and-shut case, and that the New York judiciary was highly likely to make a severe example of him to other punks with a stiff penal sentence.

The next day the good news came through that Virgin Records had paid the bail money and so Sid was released. His bail was confirmed at a 21 November hearing where the court said he was someone "who cultivates an image of antagonism and has a flagrant disregard for constitutional authority". Rumours that Mick Jagger offered to pay the bail (or, some say, was asked and declined) remained unproven. By that stage, Sid had made a press statement about Nancy: "She's in my thoughts night and day. I wake up in the night reaching out for her, for her warm body which has always been cuddled up next to me for the last two years. I get into a hot sweat because I've been dreaming. I was making love to her again. The touch of her skin floats around in my brain driving me mad. Nancy in her sexy red and black underwear, the vision of her never leaves me. I could never have killed her. When you love someone as much as I loved Nancy you could never kill her. Life's almost impossible without her. I'm constantly thinking about the good times we had together. Nancy was great because she and I were the same." That Sunday Nancy's body was buried in Philadelphia.

With Sid out on bail, there were all sorts of moves on his behalf. Malcolm McLaren had arrived over the weekend and, despite their recent falling out, was campaigning vigorously on Sid's behalf. Some cynics said he only wanted Sid on bail so he could film the events for his *Swindle* movie, but McLaren was actually disappointed when bail was granted, as he had hoped an enforced period of cold turkey on remand in the detoxification wing would help Sid's cause hugely. More days in jail for Sid would have given McLaren the time and freedom to organise the case for the defence. He seemed genuinely to feel for Sid.

Within hours of landing at New York, McLaren had approached several of America's top defence lawyers, including the famous F. Lee Bailey, who later went on to defend O. J. Simpson. After some deliberation, he engaged the major city law firm of Prior Cashman Sherman and Flynn, who estimated their legal fees would be in the region of $100,000.

No one involved had that kind of money, so McLaren put his scheming mind to ways of providing the finance. One idea was to take Sid, Cook and Jones to Miami, away from the distractions of New York, where they could record an album of family favourites like 'White Christmas' and 'Mack The Knife', and then rush-release it as a potential money-spinner. This never happened, even though Cook and Jones had no objections to helping out, a decision which cheered up Sid enormously. Some people said McLaren was trying to tie up Sid in a recording arrangement with ex-New York Doll Jerry Nolan, and he was also reported to be negotiating film and book rights to raise yet more cash. He even approached Johnny Rotten, who had no problem with helping his friend, but stipulated that he would do so only as long as McLaren wasn't present (to be fair, Rotten had his court case against McLaren impending). McLaren was not surprised by these potential offers of help from his three former colleagues. As he said to *Rolling Stone*, "They may all hate each other, but my God, you can never tell what people will do when

Anne Beverley, Sid's mother, cries outside court room when Sid's bail is revoked on 8 December.

the cards are on the table. Maybe they'll wake up to the reality of the situation and help Sid out."

While Sid's mum (who always maintained that Nancy killed herself) reportedly signed a contract for $10,000 with the suddenly interested *New York Post*, McLaren made the shrewd move of employing various private detectives to investigate the night of the murder. Within a few days they had turned up all sorts of anomalies in the apparently water-tight police case – for example, by the end of McLaren's first week, he had riddled the case for the prosecution with holes, with statements detailing at least four conflicting stories, no exact time of death, and several 'third person suspect' theories which seemed to have some credence. Sid's mother was hugely grateful for McLaren's help during this difficult period, and it has to be said that he gave Sid his best chance of avoiding being sent down. Unfortunately, McLaren's reputation went before him and some cynics saw nothing more than another Machiavellian attempt to profit from someone else's adversity. When a man has publicly declared Dickens' Scrooge amongst his all-time heroes, this kind of cynicism is understandable. However, in many senses his true motives were irrelevant, because after a few days of McLaren's concentrated efforts, Sid's cause looked much brighter.

Back in England, the Clash arranged a Sid Vicious Benefit gig at London's Music Machine venue, a show which coincided with a lower-profile Nancy Spungen Benefit at the Valentino Room in Bedford by the Cash Pussies. A short while after, Sid was voted "Best Person" and "Best Bassist" in the *NME* end-of-year polls. Meanwhile, his New York backing band were not so embroiled in their colleague's difficulties. Indeed, they took the opportunity to release a debut single and tour the UK on the wave of Sid Vicious interest. The band, calling themselves Pure Hell, toured the smaller UK circuit in November 1978.

Unfortunately, this gradual up-turn in events did little to restore Sid's crumbling state of mind. His initial confusion had evolved into despair, he was desperately missing Nancy, and with the forthcoming trial and its threat of a lengthy return to prison, he was deeply depressed. Despite McLaren's hard work, Sid was emotionally destitute. On his release on bail in the week following Nancy's death, he was given a weekend's supply of methadone, but took it all on the Friday night. By the Sunday, he was suffering severe withdrawal symptoms. It was only seven days after his release on bail, and the night after a new brace of gigs were proposed at Artemis in Philadelphia, but Sid had had enough. He took a razor blade and a broken light bulb and tried to slash his wrists, shouting, "I want to join Nancy, I didn't keep my part of the bargain."

McLaren and *NME* journalist Joe Stevens were called and raced round to the flat, where they found Sid covered in blood on the bed, urinating on himself and the blood-soaked sheets, with his mother sitting next to him doing nothing. She said simply that she felt he ought to be allowed to live out his promise to Nancy. Sid looked up in a daze and asked for some more heroin, "so I can finish the job off". McLaren said he would go to get some drugs to help Sid kill himself, but actually called an ambulance. Before it arrived, Sid tried to jump out of the window, but luckily was held back. McLaren dangled a Sex Pistols reunion as a carrot for Sid to stay alive, at least until the ambulance arrived, whereupon he was bandaged up and driven off to Bellevue Psychiatric Hospital.

After a few more days of detox at the hospital, Sid recovered and was discharged into his mother's care once again. He immediately resumed his previous New York lifestyle and even got a new girlfriend, Michelle Robinson, an unemployed actress who had already lost one boyfriend to drug excess. Although Sid spent much of his time with Robinson, it was widely seen as an emotional crutch, a selfish necessity, rather than of any romantic significance – there was never any suggestion of her usurping Nancy in his affections. Once out of Bellevue, Sid's demeanour seemed to change. His depression changed to arrogance and he became the strutting, cocky pop star who could get away with anything. Within days Sid had blown it again.

While his mother covered up for him, saying he was with her at home, Sid had been trawling round the underground of seedy New York clubs where he was obviously a freak attraction. At one of these, a new club called Hurrah's, he got into an altercation with Patti Smith's brother Todd and attacked him with a glass after first abusing his girlfriend. Smith needed five stitches. Sid was arrested and sent back to Rikers Island and suffered enforced cold turkey again. This time McLaren felt it was definitely better to let Sid stay in prison to cool off and clean up. It was now 9 December. He served another 55 days over the Christmas period in jail until his second bail was granted on 1 February 1979.

chapter 10

"I'll die before I'm very old, I don't know why, I just have this feeling."

Sid Vicious, April 1978

When Sid's second hearing for bail came up at the start of February, he was desperate to be released. McLaren was back in London fighting the impending court case brought by Johnny Rotten against McLaren's management company Glitterbest, with Rotten calling him "the most evil man alive". There were discussions aimed at settling out of court but at the last moment these failed and the date for the court hearing was set for 7 February. McLaren was further distracted by rumours circulating that Rotten's lawyers were pushing for the civil action to be followed by a criminal case. Events had also become immensely complicated by the involvement of both Warner and Virgin. As a result of this, McLaren was unable to attend Sid's own hearing in New York on 1 February – he still preferred Sid to stay in the safe confines of the jail, but the ex-Pistol pleaded with him to pay the bond. Wearily, McLaren agreed, and transferred the money across the Atlantic, so Sid was released. McLaren simply could not afford the time to be in New York with Sid when he was released the next day. This complication was to have devastating consequences.

Sid's bail was set with the condition that he was banned from clubs, discos or any gatherings where he might be tempted to repeat the Todd Smith incident. He walked out of the prison gates to be met by his mother, who had promised McLaren her son would be in safe hands, and Michelle Robinson. Sid put his arms round his mother to support himself, as he was frail, dreadfully weak and ashen grey. His grubby "I Love New York" T-shirt was only half-filled by his skeletal body and as he walked off he thrust his hands into the air in triumph. Twelve hours later he was dead.

That Sid died so soon after he was released for the second time gives some suggestion of his mental state. That he was allowed to be so openly around the drug that killed him indicates something of the environment he was in. Instead of keeping him quietly at home waiting for the trial, Sid was taken to Michelle Robinson's Greenwich Village flat for a celebration party attended by eight friends. Nancy's death was spoken about and suicide pacts were even mentioned. Sid boasted that the hard men in Rikers Island got on with him well because he was cut from the same cloth – the reality is that Sid was abused (physically and possibly sexually) and ridiculed throughout his second spell in prison, just as during the first.

As with Nancy's death, the exact chain of events is unclear, although there is far more certainty that Sid administered the fatal dose himself. After a meal of spaghetti bolognese, heroin was produced around midnight and passed around. Despite warnings that it was extremely pure, Sid was anxious to have some, so he took a fix straight away. Since he had been in prison for nearly two months and forcibly cleaned up, his body was no longer used to the drug and he almost immediately went into a seizure, with his lips turning blue and his skin taking on a grey tinge. He was taken to bed and covered with blankets, and his pulse was checked regularly until some 40 minutes later he began to revive. He was then walked around the flat until his head had cleared and he seemed to have made a reasonable recovery.

Around 3 a.m. the party finished and Michelle and Sid retired to bed. At some point Sid awoke from his slumber and injected yet more heroin, and this time there was no one awake to rouse him from his drugged sleep. His cleaned-up body could not handle the second dose and he died in the night. The following morning, Groundhog Day, his mother arose from the couch where she had slept and took two cups of tea into Sid's room. Sid lay naked on top of the covers. It was then that Anne Beverley realised her son was dead. Michelle was still asleep, unaware of her new boyfriend's death.

His mother was perplexed, because she had held the heroin that night, and knowing it was so pure she had put the remainder safely in her back pocket when the party had finished. She was unsure how Sid could have got hold of the drug. Rumours immediately started circulating that the heroin had been spiked with a poison, perhaps strychnine. This seems highly unlikely, especially as earlier that day Sid had told her, "Mum, Nancy is there on the other side waiting for me. If I'm quick, I can catch the girl I love." The suicide theory was compounded when a note was found saying, "We had a death pact, I have to keep my half of the bargain. Please bury me next to my baby. Bury me in my leather jacket, jeans and motorcycle boots. Goodbye."

McLaren had planned to fly to New York the very next day and take Sid to the safe haven of Miami, where he could immerse himself in the proposed recording sessions. Sid had been relatively healthy after his detox in prison, and there was even hope of an acquittal with all the new evidence that McLaren's legal team were unearthing. Justifiably worried that no one reliable was there to look after Sid on his release from prison, McLaren had sent Barbara Harwood, a trainee homoeopathic doctor, to look after him. However, before she could set out, she received a phone call from Sid's mother saying he was dead.

Anne Beverley had seen her son go through so much. Now he was dead she responded in *Melody Maker* in a somewhat unexpected fashion: "The day Sid died he was beautiful. He died in his sleep amongst friends. What more could you want?" She went on to say, "I'm glad he died in view of what happened. Nothing can hurt him anymore. Where could he have gone from where he was at? He was in a corner. It would have come out that it was a suicide pact, which made him guilty of manslaughter, and, sorry, here's five years... he couldn't have done that, because he was not a hard man, he was too sweet and too soft."

In the aftermath of Sid's death there was a strange period of both sorrow and exploitation. On the one hand, people who had said it was inevitable now wondered if they could have done more to stop it. On the other, the money-makers started realising the endless potential a dead Sex Pistol provided. The latter tended to be in the majority. Only three weeks after his death Virgin Records released his version of 'Something Else', backed with a Steve Jones-led rendition of 'Friggin' in the Riggin'.' Virgin claimed that the single had been previously scheduled for that release date, but having said that, schedules can always be changed. On the back of the sleeve, designer Jamie Reid wrote, "The media was our lover and helper and that in effect was the Sex Pistols' success. As today to control the media is to have the power of government, God or both." The power of the media's interest in Sid Vicious now became apparent, as the release was widely publicised and sold massively. Virgin's marketing and sales force hopes were justified as the single reached No. 3 and sold 382,000, over double the amount that 'God Save the Queen' shifted. In years to come, the cartoon Sid Vicious featured in the promo for this single became one of the most popular tattoo designs available.

His three singles were also included in the *Great Rock'n'Roll Swindle* soundtrack and Sex Pistols albums, and his own 'My Way' enjoyed rock-

SEE W IAT YOU'RE MISSING
"OBNOXIOUS"
"FILTHY LUCRE"
"POLICE SWOOP ON PUNK DISC SHOPS"
TWO FILMS FROM THE
"Fired Again"
Sex Pistols
Nu
"Foul Mouthed Yobs"
"FILTH & THE
VER MIND
Sex Pistols

Publicity material
for the film.

Chloe Webb and Gary Oldman as Nancy and
Sid in the film based on their life.

eting sales in the weeks following his death. Before the year was out Virgin had also put out *Floggin' a Dead Horse*, a Sex Pistols greatest hits package, and *Sid Sings*, an album of live material from the sub-standard Max's Kansas City gigs he performed just before Nancy's death. To ensure bad taste prevailed, a free Sid poster was given away with the album. Sid would probably have loved it.

The logical extension of the renewed fascination that Sid's premature death brought was Alex Cox's critically acclaimed 1986 movie *Sid and Nancy* (originally called *Love Kills*). Anne Beverley initially tried to prevent the film being made but once she met Cox and heard his ideas she agreed to assist on the project – Cox was already famous for his cult film *Repo Man*. He presented a script written with Abbe Wool, and Zenith Films bought the rights. The search was now on for the two key players.

Rumours had been rife in the music industry for some time that such a film was going to be made – the *NME* even advertised for Sid lookalikes to send in their photos. In the end, both actors chosen to play the central roles were relatively unknown. The part of Sid went to London-born Gary Oldman, who bore an extreme physical resemblance to the Sex Pistols bassist. It was a wise choice. Oldman applied a remarkable perfectionism to the role, starving himself down to the same scrawny frame as Sid, studiously copying his movements, accent and mannerisms. Even the padlock and chain worn around Oldman's neck was Sid's actual necklace.

This attention to detail was replicated throughout the film. With Anne Beverley on board, the background to Sid's life was exactly reproduced. Glen Matlock arranged the music, although the rest of the Sex Pistols disliked the idea and refused to co-operate. However, with the addition of Debbie Wilson, formerly of the Bromley Contingent, assisting with factual detail, and the use of some of Jamie Reid's artwork, the finished film was scrupulously detailed.

Oldman improvised heavily with the script (which he made no secret of the fact he disliked), but his fluid approach seemed to work – his on-screen relationship with Nancy, played by American Chloe Webb, was intense, powerful, and most important of all, believable. Alex Cox made full use of this celluloid chemistry, and managed to achieve his goal of focusing on the detrimental effect of drugs in the love affair, as he told *NME*: "We want to make the film, not just about Sid Vicious and punk, but as an anti-drugs statement, to show the degradation caused to various people is not at all glamorous." As a result, the closing scenes in the Chelsea Hotel are depraved, sordid and desperately depressing.

On its release, music and media magazines hailed the film's merits, with

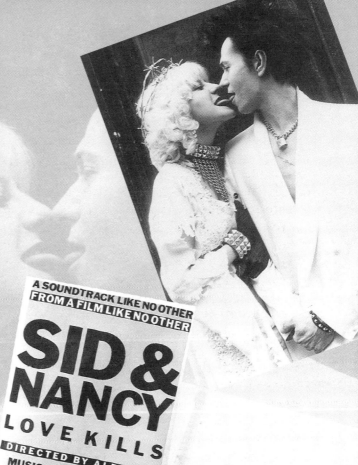

Stills from the film with
Gary Oldman as Sid and
Chloe Webb as Nancy.

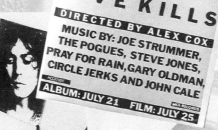

A SOUNDTRACK LIKE NO OTHER
FROM A FILM LIKE NO OTHER

SID &
NANCY

LOVE KILLS

DIRECTED BY ALEX COX

MUSIC BY: JOE STRUMMER,
THE POGUES, STEVE JONES,
PRAY FOR RAIN, GARY OLDMAN,
CIRCLE JERKS AND JOHN CALE

ALBUM: JULY 21   FILM: JULY 25

MCA RECORDS

Rolling Stone and *The Los Angeles Times* being just two examples of the American heavyweight support. In the UK, the *Mail on Sunday* called it "a savagely brilliant account of the last days of Sid Vicious". The praise was justified – Alex Cox accurately portrayed the rollercoaster ride of Sid and Nancy's love affair, from the passionate euphoria of their early love, through to the sheer hell of their heroin fuelled self-destruction. After watching *Sid and Nancy*, compelled by the spiralling depths of the portrayed drug addiction, the viewer can only agree with Anne Beverley's epitaph to the film, as she told Alan Parker in his book *Sid's Way*: "They were a modern day Romeo and Juliet...if ever two people shouldn't have met it was Sime and Nancy."

Back in 1979, this was all a long way off. Sid was cremated in New York, the city that had fascinated him so much that it had eventually drawn him to his early demise. At first, his dying wish to have his ashes sprinkled on Nancy's grave were denied when the Spungen family refused to reveal where she was buried. Even in death Sid Vicious continued to confuse. Some claimed that Sid's mother finally found out the location of the Jewish cemetery where Nancy was located and carried out her son's last wish. Other reports in the tabloids suggested that the casket containing his ashes was, in fact, dropped and smashed on the floor of Heathrow airport, only to be swept up and disposed of in a fittingly farcical ending.

Whatever became of Sid's remains, questions began to be asked about what could have been done to save him. Fingers of blame were pointed in various directions as people tried to make sense of what had been an almost inevitable conclusion to two years of escalating self-destruction.

In the first instance, Sid's friends at the party were lambasted for not protecting him sufficiently from heroin, at a time when they knew he was particularly vulnerable. All reports suggest it was freely available, very pure and, after so long without it, doubly dangerous. His mother, loyal to the last, could also be criticised for her part. She never chastised Sid, never gave him any parameters to stay within, and the resulting free licence he indulged in took him to his grave. On the night of his death, she was the one holding the heroin. Vivienne Westwood had always felt Anne spoilt Sid, like many one-child families do, saying she supported his lies while on bail just as she helped him do drugs. Sid used to shoot up heroin in front of her almost as a challenge to her parental authority. Some said that Sid never grew out of his childhood, that he was a young impressionable mind thrust into a violent and dangerous arena, with no one there to check his activities.

The aftermath of the
Sex Pistols.

Having said all that, Anne Beverley was always behind Sid, she never questioned him, never let him down and would drop everything to be at his side in times of need. During a childhood that was fragmented, insecure and at times traumatic, Anne succeeded in bringing some stability and identity into Sid's life. She was a far more loving mother and friend than many people ever have. It was just unfortunate that one of the indulgences she and Sid shared helped to kill him.

Many bitter voices talked of Malcolm McLaren's role. He had recruited Sid into the Sex Pistols in the first place and had played on his weak character, encouraging increasingly more depraved behaviour, so that by the time the US tour ended Sid had reached a dangerous peak of excess. He played on Sid's lack of personal confidence and his inability to form his own character, and shaped him into a punk cliché that was exceptionally bankable. As Johnny Rotten gradually proved more and more difficult, Sid remained an easily manipulated puppet, a figurehead for McLaren's revolution. Having said that, McLaren also helped Sid, intentionally or otherwise, during the dark days in Rikers Island, and that should not be forgotten. Malcolm McLaren later said of Sid in *The Wicked Ways of Malcolm McLaren*: "Sid was a guy who never saw any sense of danger, a real street kid who never saw a red light. He was always the ultimate believer in the Sex Pistols' ideas and attitudes... long after Rotten had become a bit of a joke, very serious, very career minded." McLaren was bitterly disappointed that Sid did not fulfil what he saw as great potential, as he told the music press at the time: "Sid showed what a good voice he had for that band and things were looking very good for him. To me he was the archetypal punk, and someone I had great respect for. I think he had a lot of people he could reach out and communicate with from the stage, and I still think he had great potential."

Johnny Rotten (now Lydon again), Sid's best friend, has since openly admitted that he has retraced his part in the tragedy many times, wondering if he could have behaved differently. It was not as if he didn't try at all, however. He tired of Sid's continued abuse and did try to help him off drugs several times, but once Sid was with Nancy, Rotten no longer felt the bond of friendship was there: "His attitude changed completely when he met Nancy. He was banging up all day and night. He became a total bore and just didn't recognise anyone anymore. It was pathetic." Despite this, Rotten never assuaged the guilt he felt for pushing Nancy on to Sid in the first instance, and later felt he could have done more, as he said in his autobiography: "If only I hadn't been lazy and washed my hands of him like Pontius Pilate. That's something I'll have to carry to the grave with me. I don't know what I could have done but I should have done something. There are always ways. You must never be lazy when it comes to your friends."

Then there was Nancy, the wicked witch of the piece. Her premature death had surprised many people, who had suspected that Sid would die first, after which Nancy would just move on to another gullible star. She preyed on Sid's weaknesses to achieve her own ends, she manipulated him and alienated all his close friends, all the people who might have stopped his decline. She was persistently dishonest with him, and deep down Sid knew this. She introduced him to his heroin habit, she contributed to the break-up of the band that was his passion and she took him back to New York, filling his head with ideas that were to be utterly destructive. She convinced him that to be a true rock'n'roll star, he had to play the dangerous drugs game. Indirectly, once she had gone, her hold on his mind was so complete that Sid went into a shock from which he never recovered, and her death was the immediate catalyst for his own demise. She must carry a heavy burden of responsibility.

After Sid's death, Nancy's family received scores of obscene phone calls from distraught Sid fans who berated Nancy's parents for not using contraceptives to prevent their daughter ever being born. In punk circles, and especially amongst Sid's close friends, Nancy was seen as instrumental in Sid's death, to the extent that many people were of the opinion that, had he not met her, he would still be alive today. Many felt they had never had the chance to see Sid with good friends around him, people who would look after him, because Nancy was always there, corrupting him constantly.

On the other hand, Nancy and Sid clearly loved each other. Despite their frequent fights and damaging mutual habits, the pair were devoted to each other and provided close comfort and company at many difficult times. When Sid was in hospital with hepatitis, Nancy was the only regular visitor he had and he never forgot that – she was his ally, his friend and his lover. They shared the same outlook on life and he worshipped her. He once said, "Nancy was great because she and I were the same, we both hated everyone." Whatever anyone else thought of her, Nancy Spungen was the light of Sid Vicious' life.

The media were blamed in some quarters, for elevating a nobody to a lofty star status that he patently could not handle, with the only logical conclusion being his early death. The Sex Pistols played a game with the media, and Sid desperately wanted to be seen by the press and public alike as the personification of the Sex Pistols. Even when the band had split, he sought to maintain that image, despite the newspapers' rapidly dwindling interest in him. Sid was a media creation in some ways, with the enormous amount of mythologising that sprang up around him and is still there to this day. Sid fell to what became punk's in-built drive to oblivion. With the dying embers of punk rock cooling at the end of the seventies, heroin swept through the punk has-beens, convincing them they were still somebody. Sid fell for this trap and it destroyed him.

At the same time, many of the elements of Sid Vicious were very real, very much of his own making. One of those elements was his self-destructive impulse. Sid's musical contribution to the Sex Pistols was zero, so he compensated for this by contributing to the visual circus. As his lack of musicianship grew ever more apparent, he made up for it with increasingly gross acts of anarchy and self-mutilation, slashing himself with broken bottles, appearing for interviews smashed on dope, fighting needlessly – anything that might elevate him to the status of a punk rock hero. He openly admitted he cut himself as a release of this frustration: "Everything is done when I get so annoyed over something so much that I need an enemy... and I always find that I'm sitting in a room with a load of friends and I can't do anything to them, so I just go upstairs and smash a glass and cut myself. And then I feel better."

Then there was Sid's fundamental character. Poor old Sid. Vivienne Westwood always sympathised with him, as she told Craig Bromberg in his book, *The Wicked Ways of Malcolm McLaren*: "Sid didn't know bad from good. He didn't know right from wrong most of the time, that boy. He just didn't have an ego, especially not about wanting to perform, even though he was a natural performer. He was just a very affectionate, very intelligent, very funny, warm person." So he was too dumb to make up his own mind, yet friends claimed he was sharp, witty and highly intelligent. When Rotten first met him, he was consumed with David Bowie, suffering an impulse to imitate. Rotten had nothing but contempt for this desire to copy others, even when he was the subject of that imitation himself, as he told *Trouser Press* magazine: "I don't like walking the streets and seeing three thousand imitations of me, that pisses me off, quite frankly. I always used to laugh looking at all the Bowie imitators, all the Bryan Ferry imitators. It was just a joke, people without minds of their own, or directions or anything. The great unthinking majority." Sid was very much a part of this unthinking majority – he aped Dee Dee Ramone and did not sway from this admiration even when the Ramones announced they did not like him or the Sex Pistols. Sid seemed unable throughout his life to acquire an identity of his own. Whereas great performers take elements of others and mould something new, Sid just stole blatantly and clumsily. Even his trademark leather jacket was nothing new.

For many observers the drugs took a large slice of the blame. Apparently he was funny, goofy and sweet before the heroin, an animal afterwards; perceptive before, stupid after. Rotten said in his autobiography, "Sid was naive but full of wit about things. Excellent person, but drugs did him in and turned him into a deeply unpleasant Mr Hyde." However, Sid was injecting speed and assaulting people way before he met Nancy or shot heroin. True, he was young, but at 19 he knew he was taking the heroin, he knew he was doing the things he did to himself and to others. Other heroin addicts used the drug and didn't do the things that Sid did. He knew that after every detox he would end up back on the stuff and he chose to do that.

There were other elements of Sid's character that contributed to his downfall. His obsession with his looks, which had started with his varnished toenails, dominated every aspect of his life. Even in New York, when he was fearfully thin and hideously drug-riddled, he would look in the mirror to check his hair or adjust his clothes. As his fame grew, Sid's vanity swelled, and with that the desire to present the ultimate punk rock vision and his absolute need to be noticed became predominant. In many ways, he was noticed, but it cost him dear. His lack of identity meant he would always follow the crowd, and it is ironic that he made perhaps his only memorable musical contribution with the single 'My Way', singing lyrics which bore little relation to his approach to life.

There were other players in the death of Sid Vicious. There were people who could have helped but didn't, others who deliberately added to his downfall. Ultimately, however, Sid was his own worst enemy. The person most responsible for Sid Vicious' death was Sid Vicious.

From an obscure hanger-on to a dead punk-rock icon, Sid Vicious' time in the spotlight was only 21 months, just one month for each year of his life. In that time, his close friends saw his mental and physical health deteriorate dramatically, while his fame and notoriety rocketed. Some said that he ruined the Sex Pistols, that they never produced the same greatness once he had joined and started to screw up. Others believe Sid Vicious was the single most interesting element in the whole Pistols story. Similarly, by the time Sid was dead, punk rock itself had become absorbed into the mainstream with major acts selling millions of records and the more acceptable term 'new wave' being used to quantify the left-overs – punk's radical beginnings had been hijacked by the mainstream for the benefit of mass consumerism. Punk fragmented in the months following the Sex Pistols' break-up, but for many it was more specific than that – Sid's death heralded the final nail in punk's coffin.

Since his death, Sid's role in punk and in the Sex Pistols has been documented, distorted, fabricated and generally mythologised. Some twenty years later, when the band reformed for their 1996 anniversary tour, Johnny Rotten was less charitable about his former friend. At the press conference to announce their return, Rotten told the waiting media, "Even if Sid was still around, it [the reunion tour] would have to be with Glen. Sid actually did nothing. Sid was a coathanger. It's unfortunate that as the years have gone by, the rumour mongers, liars and ex-managers have managed to blow out of all proportion and take away from what was real. Sid's been cloned and the arseholes and morons have bought that imagery totally, lock, stock and barrel. It was never about studded leather jackets and black biker boots. I mean, that's dull, that's the clichés and trappings of everything that was in rock'n'roll before we started. So when I see gangs of punks running around in studded leather jackets these days, I just get sick. They got it wrong. They can wear all that stuff by all means, but don't be calling yourselves no punks... People seem to have built this huge myth around him and that's all well and fine cos it's funny. But they should know that that's all it is. A myth."

The other members of the Sex Pistols survived through self-preservation, persistence, a degree of emotional stability and luck. Sid had none of these. Sid became a twisted punk myth, as Rotten says, and aged just 21 he entered the rock'n'roll hall of fame. Like that other leather-jacketed rebel, James Dean, Sid Vicious burned out early. He was always telling Glen Matlock he would die by the time he was 21, and regularly claimed to have had premonitions of his death. When it finally came true, Sid had already written his own epitaph, having told an interviewer in January 1978, "I'll die before I'm 25, and when I do I'll have lived the way I wanted to."

Epilogue

Two days after this book was completed, Anne Beverley was found dead from an overdose of painkillers and alcohol at her home in South Derbyshire. She was 64. Police were alerted after a neighbour received a letter from Anne, shortly after returning from her summer holiday, announcing her intention to take her own life. Although her body was still warm when the police entered the house, all attempts at resuscitation failed. She was buried that week at a small and very quiet funeral. A precise will had been left with a solicitor in nearby Burton.

Next to the body, police found her credit cards cut in half and various bags of her clothes nearby. Strewn on the floor were half-spilt bottles of diazepam and codamol painkillers, as well as an empty vodka bottle. In a glass cabinet in the room, a velvet cushion caressed a cherished memento of her son's life – a small padlock on a short but heavy metal chain.

Some years ago, Anne Beverley had fled London to find a peaceful new life in the quiet former mining village of Swadlincote, where few of the unassuming neighbours knew of her famous son. Her house was ideal for such a retreat, a mundane affair in an uneventful town. From here she managed Sid's estate, and proved annoyingly intransigent for various record company executives to deal with. Back at home, her two dogs and a handful of friends were her only company.

In 1986, she had received around £250,000 as Sid's share of an out-of-court settlement between Malcolm McLaren and the Sex Pistols, and an additional £100,000 a year in royalties since then. Despite this financial windfall, all was not well. The long-term back pain from which she suffered had recently worsened and was exacerbated by one single event – the Sex Pistols reunion tour. Her son had been replaced by his predecessor, and his memory tarnished when the band talked of Sid as just a useless hanger-on. She publicly defended her son and berated his former colleagues, but her rantings were largely ignored. By the middle of the year, she had had enough.

In addition to the toxins in her bloodstream, there was a broken needle still in her arm, which doctors had previously been unable to remove. It was a small reminder of the drug that had dominated much of her life and the final years of Sid's.

Perhaps with her death the story will finally come to a close.